F. W. Webb

1836 - 1906

A Bibliography

John E. Spink

Preface to the Reprint

John E. Spink's bibliography of F. W. Webb has been known to students of the LNWR for many years, probably almost since a copy was first deposited in Crewe Library, and has been greatly admired and respected.

So when Peter Stanton, chairman of the LNWR Society, obtained a copy, it was not difficult to suggest that it should be reprinted for the benefit of members of the LNWR Society and others who might be interested. The proposal found total support in the committee, a professional typist was employed to re-type the text (many thanks to Mrs Margaret Gladwin), photographs were obtained from the Society's archives, others were taken specially for the purpose, and this book is the result.

John Spink's original text appears here as it does in the original thesis. Three items of 'Additional material', which were obtained after the main body of the thesis had been typed and were added at the end, have been incorporated into the appropriate places in the text but have not been altered in any way. Otherwise, no changes whatsoever have been made to his text.

Fortunately, interest in the LNWR and in F. W. Webb has not declined over the intervening years since Spink's bibliography was first completed, and quite possibly is greater than it has ever been. Only four years ago John Chacksfield's biography of Webb was published, and it is hoped that the publication of Spink's bibliography may stimulate further research and the publication of further biographical works on the great man.

Edward Talbot
Gnosall
Stafford
August 2011

Finding John E. Spink

The copy of the book that led to this Society publication has an interesting little story behind it!

My good friend, Martyn Chapman, always comes up with interesting ideas for my birthday present and thought he had really scored when he found a bound volume entitled *F. W. Webb* in a box under the table at a Swapmeet. He was even more taken when he found it was a bound carbon of a dissertation and therefore almost unique!

I soon enjoyed the ownership of the tome and when I took it to the late Peter Turville's At Home realised just how much interest there was in it; my friends couldn't put it down. John Chacksfield then borrowed it and used some of the content in his book on the great man.

I talked to Ted Talbot about it and we felt that here was an opportunity that should not be missed by our membership, to share in the enjoyment of Mr Spink's work.

We then had to gain the author's permission to publish. The book contained a copy of a letter to the British Library Society covering the submission but when I spoke to the successor to that Society there was no news of Mr Spink. Mrs Lynne Chapman, however, is a Chartered Librarian and took up the search through her professional contacts: Lo and behold, in a couple of weeks I had an address for Mr Spink. I wrote to him and received a prompt response, mainly full of amazement! He was really pleased to think that we wished to publish and readily gave us his blessing!

So there is the story behind our latest publication; I hope you all enjoy it!

Peter Stanton.
Chairman,
London & North Western Railway
Society

Reply from John E. Spink

Dear Peter Stanton

Delighted, no less, to learn that you wish to publish my 1965 thesis on F. W. Webb. If you circulate it to rail enthusiasts, it will be a tribute to the many Crewe people who helped me. It will also be a tribute to my supervisor, the late George Ottley (author, among other works, of the *Bibliography of British Railway History*, 1966).

Thus you have my agreement to publish but you may need approval from the CILIP (Chartered Institute of Library and Information Professionals), formerly the Library Association.

The thesis is cited in the Webb entry in the *Oxford Companion to British Railways* of 1997, where I appear incorrectly as J. F. Spink. My thesis, though it was written with enthusiasm, must be very dated and may contain inaccuracies. You may, of course, make these.

I gave my collection of photographs and relevant papers to Crewe Public Libraries. It may be worth looking at them with a view to adding pictures. I hope they still have them.

Now, approaching 80, I feel that I have left Webb far behind; but then I realise that I sit daily with a picture of *Hardwicke* (No. 790) in front of me, and then remember that last year my wife and I visited *Hardwicke* at the York Railway Museum.

Yours sincerely
John E. Spink

F. W. Webb

1836 - 1906

A Bibliography

Francis William Webb,
Chief Mechanical Engineer,
London & North Western Railway, 1871-1903:
a survey of material for a study of his life and
work.

Thesis submitted for the
Fellowship of the Library Association,
October, 1965.

John E. Spink

Published by the
London & North Western Railway
Society

Contents

'You will have me admire a steam-engine. Why? Because of its delicately adjusted mechanism, its perfect adaptation to modern needs. So be it. I will modify my conception of what is fair in appearance. I will admire your steam-engine, and thereby bring my ideals of beauty up to date'.

Norman Douglas, *South Wind*, Chapter 38

Preface

There is a cruel irony in the fact that, at a time when our railway system is undergoing severe pruning, the history of railways is receiving livelier and fuller treatment than ever before. H. J. Dyos has noted that one of the characteristics of transport history 'is the rather dessicated air which much of it has, as the result of inordinate emphasis having been laid on the evolution of the means of transport itself – locomotive, ship, aeroplane or road vehicle – to the general neglect till comparatively recently of the economic and social aspects'.[1]

Fortunately a number of historians have gathered around Leicester University's *Journal of Transport History* and have altered this situation as far as the railway is concerned. Michael Robbins, himself a member of this group, has noted the new movement: 'Perhaps the most encouraging thing about the practice of railway history in the past ten years or so has been a genuine attempt to seek out new evidence, to probe fresh sources, and to bring a more vigorously critical approach to bear on the traditional accounts'.[2]

Some would say that it is too late, that too much evidence, especially that in brick and iron, has gone. However, the existence of new material and new approaches has been successfully demonstrated in at least two books, Professor Simmon's *The Railways of Britain* (1961) and Michael Robbins's *The Railway Age* (1962), and in numerous articles.

The new writers have tended, quite logically, to concentrate on the early period of railway history, and it has been my aim to apply their approach to a study in the 'middle' period.

My plan has been to provide complete bibliographies, missing out only the slightest references and news items, covering every aspect of the life and work of F. W. Webb. These I have prefaced by essays which are a convenient way of drawing attention to brief references which do not have a place in the bibliographies, and which have been planned to demonstrate the general scope of each topic while emphasising those aspects which have received little attention.

Michael Robbins has said, 'The kind of railway history I want is accurate, comprehensive, and readable. That is all'.[3] How far I have succeeded will depend upon how far I have supplied these admirable requirements.

This study has not been without its disappointments. At an early stage I was precluded from airing some of my theories in *The Railway Magazine* by the appearance of two articles on Webb by J. M. Dunn. The disappointment was slight, however, for the articles are a real contribution to the subject and everyone interested in the LNWR must be pleased to see them in print.

I will mention my debt to Mr Dunn later. I was to find, also, that Professor Foxwell's description of the LNWR in the 1880s had already been used by Mr O. S. Nock in his *Race to the North*. I have retained the quotation, however, for it is a splendid summary.

I have not seen all the material that I would like to have consulted. It has not been possible for me to search all the North American and Continental periodicals that I would like to have done, and I am sorry that more new material, especially letters and official documents, did not come to light.

Despite these disappointments, I have obtained a great deal of pleasure from working on this thesis. Any piece of work which requires one to read books and articles by such writers as W. H. Acworth, E. L. Ahrons and J. G. B. Sams is certain to give the researcher an enviable task.

Nothing, however, has given me greater pleasure than the friendliness and willing assistance that I have received from so many people during my work. I must particularly thank my supervisor, Mr George Ottley, who has been kept very busy by this task while at the same time making his own far greater contribution to railway hstory, and Mr J. M. Dunn for his great kindness in lending me all the notes for his *Railway Magazine* articles. His genealogical researches are fully described in my thesis and the section on Webb's patents is based entirely on his work. It was his assistance which set me so confidently on my task.

Many thanks are also due to Dr W. H. Chaloner (who gave me access to his fine collection of Crewe material), Mr Arthur Jameson (a former LNWR driver who sent me some stirring accounts of footplate work), Mr William Pover (who did much valuable 'field-work'), Mr Geoffrey Nulty (who guided me through the *Crewe Guardian*), Mr F. A. S. Brown (who introduced me to Peter Taylor), Mr Neil Fraser (for material on the 'Intimidation Affair'), the BTC Archivist, the librarians and their staffs at the Institution of Civil Engineers, the Institution of Mechanical Engineers, the Iron and Steel Institute (who performed an important service by keeping my enquiry 'active' for over a year), and the public libraries of Swindon, Bournemouth, Crewe and Bolton. Thanks also to the various people at Crewe Works who gave such willing help, especially Messrs Moulton and Rice and 'Ernie' Dutton.

Mr Malcolm Lewis spared much time to discuss many aspects of my work and now knows far more about F. W. Webb than he ever wanted to know. Mr Neil Cossons, of Bristol Museum, gave me great assistance and critically reviewed the final draft.

It will be remembered that E. Nesbit's *Railway Children* found 'everybody that has anything to do with railways is so kind and good'.[1] The passage of time and great changes on the railways - since 1906 when those words were written – have not changed the attitude of railway enthusiasts.

(1) *Library Association Record*, Vol 59 (1957), p 388-92
(2) *Journal of Transport History*, Vol 3 (1957), p 65: Michael Robbins, 'What kind of railway history do we want?'
(3) *Journal of Transport History*, Vol 3 (1957), p 75.
(1) Penguin Books edition, p 78

Finally I would note that my interest in the LNWR has not ceased with the completion of this thesis. I hope that anyone who shares my enthusiasm, especially if he has a bundle of Webb letters, will get in touch with me.

Hereford College of Education,
College Road,
HEREFORD.

John E. Spink

January 1965.

Abbreviations

London & North Western Railway has throughout been abbreviated to LNWR.

Roman numerals have been converted to Arabic numerals except in the case of pagination where preliminary pages are indicated by roman numerals.

Ahrons, *BSRL* – Ahrons, E. L., *The British Steam Railway Locomotive, 1825-1925* Locomotive Pub Co, 1927.
Ahrons, *LTWNC* – Ahrons, E. L., *Locomotive and Train Working in the Latter Part of the Nineteenth Century. Vol.1.*
BRBHR - British Railway Board Historical Records.
Chaloner - Chaloner, W. H. *The Social and Economic Development of Crewe, 1870-1923*, Manchester UP, 1950.
CC - *Crewe Chronicle.*
CG - *Crewe Guardian.*
ICE - Minutes of proceedings of the Institution of Civil Engineers.
IMechE – Proceedings of the Institution of Mechanical Engineers.
ISI - *The Journal of the Iron and Steel Institute.*
LRCWR - *Locomotive Railway Carriage and Wagon Review.*
RCHS - *The Journal of the Railway and Canal Historical Society.*
Steel - Steel, Wilfred L. *The History of the London and North Western Railway*, Railway and Travel Monthly, 1914.
SLS - *Journal of the Stephenson Locomotive Society.*

Incomplete references have been given in round brackets, for example, where dated press-cuttings have been seen and no files of the periodical have been traced in this country.

1a - The Importance of F. W. Webb

*'So many books have already been written about locomotives that an
additional work on the subject demands some apology for its appearance.'*

These words were written by C. J. Bowen Cooke in the preface to his book *British Locomotives* which was published in 1893. If an apology for another railway book was necessary then, it would appear that it is even more necessary over half a century later. Despite all the attention given to railway history, however, most writers seem to be content to re-tell the well known stories (the Rainhill Trials, the Battle of the Gauges, the Railway Race to the North, and so on) and to avoid the labour of re-examining and re-assessing the work of the engineers. There are some notable exceptions: L. T. C. Rolt has written authoritative works on some of the pioneers (Brunel and the Stephensons), and there are a few studies of the twentieth-century engineers, F. A. S. Brown's book on Sir Nigel Gresley being an example.

It is surprising that the engineers of the 'Middle Period' (between the pioneers and the engineers of this century, roughly 1860 to 1910) have received so little serious study. Such men as Adams, Dean, the Drummonds, S. W. Johnson, David Jones, the Stirlings, Stroudley and the rest, have colourful personalities and belong to a vital time in railway history. The period of construction and amalgamation was over: 'By 1870 the railway system was all but stabilised. The London & North Western, in length of line and relations with its neighbours, had become very much what it remained when welded into the London Midland & Scottish of 1923'. [1]

There was now a period of fierce competition between the companies, each of which struggled to provide faster, cheaper and more comfortable travel for its passengers, more economical ways of building and running engines, and bigger profits for the shareholders. Something of the excitement of the period can be seen in the gaiety of the company liveries and the variety of the engine names. Something of the character of the period has been faithfully portrayed in Professor Foxwell's contemporary description of the LNWR:

'The North-Western has a perfect permanent way, with very easy gradients (except between Preston and Carlisle), and Mr Webb's superb "compound" engines have lately been pouring out in quantities regardless of cost; the rolling-stock is probably the best in the kingdom; the company holds the preference share of our richest traffic, and its revenue is indeed "princely" (given as £11,000,000 per annum). We merely remark that its average speed is not quite up to the level of all this splendour and prestige. Except in this one item, there is no doubt that the North-Western is "the leading line". And in the vital matter of punctuality this company easily carries off the prize; its arrivals are a lesson to the Midland or small delinquents north of the

(1) J. H. Clapham, *An Economic History of Modern Britain*, Vol 2 (1932) p185.

Thames ... Hence, business people are strongly prejudiced in favour of the North-Western as against alternative routes; and in consequence its carriages are on the average more crowded than those of any other trunk line. North-Western porters and guards do their work with military precision, but with a finished nonchalance which is appropriate to the oldest and most punctual of our great companies'. [1]

Francis William Webb of Crewe is a key figure in this period. At a time when all chief mechanical engineers were very powerful [2], he was remarkable for the high position and autonomy that he commanded in the LNWR. Having wide responsibilities, and receiving the handsome annual salary of £7,000 [3] – more, it is said, than the General Manager – he governed 18,000 men, nearly a third of the Company's employees [4], and had great influence in a town of 28,761. [5] His company wanted economies, and Webb organised what was then the largest factory in the world so that cheap, reliable engines could be produced quickly. This was achieved by the use of cheaper materials, production-line methods of construction, and the use of standardised components. Unfortunately, however, his most ambitious attempt to economise, the application of the compounding principle to locomotive engines, was not a great success.

Webb also illustrates the transitional nature of the period. He had the inventive genius which one associates with the pioneer engineers, but while prepared to try many new ideas (double-chimneys, compounding, combustion chambers, use of steel for boilers, etc) he had a life-long distrust of the bogie and a strange reverence for the single-driver, which made him sceptical about the value of coupling driving wheels.

He has suffered at the hands of the popularisers more than any other engineer; using a few oft-told tales – the 'Take him out, bring him round, and sack him' story and a few more – they have reduced his character and career to a stereotyped 'legend'. [6] This may be summarised in Sellar and Yeatman fashion thus:

1. The 'Jumbos' – a good thing.
2. The compounds – a bad thing.
3. His autocratic character – a very bad thing.

These three points are repeated by writer after writer with little re-examination of the facts. The summaries

(1) E. Foxwell and T. C. Farrer, *Express Trains: English and Foreign* (1889), p11-2.
(2) These late Victorian CMEs are eulogised by C. Hamilton Ellis in *British Railway History, 1877-1947* (1959), p356-7.
(3) *CC*, 14th March 1903, p8.
(4) *CC*, 9th June 1906, p5.
(5) Population figure for 1891: Chaloner, p287.
(6) O. S. Nock, *British Steam Railways* (1961), p184: 'Idiosyncracies have become a legend to be retold, and exaggerated, by nearly everyone who takes up paper and pen to write about Crewe of the late nineteenth century.'

of his character are monotonous in their similarity. O. S. Nock finds him 'an unapproachable martinet' [1], C Hamilton Ellis 'severe autocracy personified' [2], Canon Roger Lloyd 'the unchallenged and unchallengeable dictator who revelled in his power' [3], while H. M. Le Fleming notes his 'autocratic manner and resentment of suggestion' [4]. That Webb was autocratic cannot be denied, that he was even more autocratic than his fellow CMEs is likely, but there were explanations for his character and there were other aspects of it; these are rarely noted. His autocratic manner is always mentioned, less frequent reference is made to his life-long fear of mental illness, his generosity, his recognition of ability (seen in the career of Mr Dick [5]), his interest in technical education, and the generally happy atmosphere in the works.

Canon Roger Lloyd and C. Hamilton Ellis give the impression that life in the works was sheer hell and that Webb was perpetually the stern man portrayed in the photographs. The latter writer uses such expressions as 'secret police methods' [6], 'coercion' and 'intimidation' [7] to describe Webb's activities and Dr Chaloner has described the 'Intimidation Affair' at Crewe. [8] It would be wrong to emphasise Webb's opposition to Liberalism and the railway unions, however, for when viewed in relation to his Company's opposition, and indeed the opposition of all the railway companies, Webb's part is seen as a very minor one. The situation is put into perspective by reading such books as *Amalgamated Society of Railway Servants: Souvenir History* (1910), Rowland Kenney's *Men and Rails* (1913), G. D. H. Cole and R. Page Arnot's *Trade Unionism on the Railways* (1917), G. W. Alcock's *Fifty Years of Railway Trade Unionism* (1922), G. C. Halverson's thesis *The Development of Labour Relations in the British Railways since 1860* [9], Philip S. Bagwell's *The Railwaymen: the history of the National Union of Railwaymen* (1963). These reveal the long and bitter opposition of the unions; there is no reference to the Crewe affair in any of them. That working conditions were slow to improve can be seen by reading Alfred Williams's account of Swindon Works, *Life in a Railway Factory*; Williams was employed at Swindon from 1892 until 1914.

In contrast to the retroactive impressions of life in Crewe Works we have a contemporary picture provided by J. G. B. Sams, who worked there during Webb's time: 'I got plenty of ... heavy work, as I was fairly heavily built, but I must say that we were not expected to work very hard at it. There were always three hands on

this section, an apprentice who was always a bird of passage, and two regular erectors named Walton and Capper, the latter being a crack Bisley shot and not too frightfully fond of work. He was easily the most amusing man that I met in the whole works.' [1]

This passage does not suggest that life under Webb was very hard or that his workmen were cowed or submissive.

That Webb had a lighter side to his character is shown in a curious incident during the opening ceremony of Queen's Park. It was baldly reported in the *Crewe Guardian* thus: 'The MAYOR [ie Webb] then addressed the public assembled from the steps of the orchestra, saying: "Gentlemen, - I am now in command. (Laughter). This park has been given to Crewe, and you must please take your cue from me (Renewed laughter)".' [2]

It is surprising that the critics of Webb do not draw attention to the high accident rate on the railways. Dr Bagwell notes that 'in the quarter century between 1875 and 1899, no less than 12,870 railwaymen were killed and 68,575 were injured', [3] and shunting accidents had become so alarming by 1879 that they were the subject of comment in a *Punch* cartoon headed 'Five thousand shunting accidents in five years'. [4]

In his *Railway Magazine* interview Webb said, 'We make all sorts of things in Crewe Works – down to artificial legs and arms for the poor fellows who lose their limbs by accident in the service of the LNWR'. [5] That these were not merely occasional manufactures is shown by Acworth who noted that 'two men are constantly employed making artificial limbs.' [6] Webb was as responsible for the dangerous working conditions as he was for the hostile attitude of railway management to the unions.

One aspect of Webb's work which has received little attention is his encouragement of technical education. He actively supported Crewe Mechanics' Institution, teaching there between 1851 and 1866 [7], and later taking a leading part in its expansion. Through his efforts ten new class-rooms were added in 1880 and there was a further addition in 1902. [8] A new physical laboratory was built in 1903. [9] The success of the Institution can be gauged from the fact that between 1872 and 1909 its students gained fifty-three Whitworth awards: 'Webb, the local patriot *par excellence*, calculated that on the basis of population, Crewe was only entitled to one Whitworth award in a century'. [10] Webb would clearly have appreciated the Crewe

(1) O. S. Nock, *LNWR* (1960), p59.
(2) C. Hamilton Ellis, *The Trains We Loved* (1947), p30.
(3) Roger Lloyd, *Railwaymen's Gallery* (1953), p113.
(4) H. M. Le Fleming in *Concise Encyclopaedia of World Railway Locomotives* (1959), p502.
(5) G. P. Neale, *Railway Reminiscences* (1904, p217.
(6) C. Hamilton Ellis, *Twenty Locomotive Men* (1958), p146.
(7) C. Hamilton Ellis, *British Railway History, 1877-1947*, p19.
(8) W. H. Chaloner, p147-66, 308-10.
(9) PhD thesis of the University of London, 1952.

(1) *Railway Magazine*, Vol 54 (1924), p383-4.
(2) *Jubilee of Crewe* (1887, p88.
(3) Philip S. Bagwell, *The Railwaymen*, p95.
(4) *Punch*, Vol 76 (1879), p135
(5) *Railway Magazine*, Vol 6 (1900), p104.
(6) W. H. Acworth, *The Railways of England*, (5th ed, 1900), p 62.
(7) W. H. Chaloner, p238.
(8) *ibid*, p237.
(9) *ibid*, p246.
(10) W. H. Chaloner, p244-5.

Locomotive Works Training School which was opened in September 1955.

Mention is made in the Minutes of the Locomotive and Engineering Committee of the LNWR of a 'Scientific Society formed by Mr Webb some years ago, the members consisting principally of Draughtsmen and Foremen'. At this committee meeting (March, 1901) permission was given for the society to hold meetings in the 'Old Hospital'. At a later meeting (August, 1902) these premises were reported to be unsuitable as vibration set up by traffic on the Liverpool line was affecting instructions.

Mention should also be made of some of the men who received training from Webb. Sir Nigel Gresley spent the first five years of his working life (1893-1898) as a pupil of Webb [1], Alexander McDonnell served with him before going to Ireland, John Aspinall (subsequently CME of the L&YR) trained under him and was promoted by him to Manager of the Crewe steelworks [2], and George Hughes (the last CME of the L&YR and the first CME of the LMS) trained under him in the 1880s. [3] H. A. Ivatt, whose greatest work was to be done on the GNR, trained under Webb and later, on the Great Southern & Western Railway of Ireland, experimented with compounding. [4] The Worsdell Brothers both worked for Webb. T. W. Worsdell had two periods at Crewe, the last of which, spent as Works Manger, prepared him for his compounding work on the North Eastern Railway. His first design for the NER, a 2-4-2 tank engine built in March 1886, shows obvious Webb influence: it has Webb radial axle-boxes and Joy valve gear. [5]

Webb did not forget education in his will. He left money for the founding of scholarships at the universities of Manchester and Liverpool, and for the establishment of an Institution of Civil Engineers prize for papers on railway engineering.

Yet another aspect of Webb's work that has received little attention is his energetic publicising of the engineering aspects of the LNWR. He never missed an opportunity to provide the press with details of new locomotives: photographs from the department of Mr Slight and running details to show the efficiency of his compounds. All the compounds appeared 'to the accompaniment of pompously powerful publicity' [6] but the climax was reached when *Greater Britain* emerged from the works: 'no other engine ever received so much attention either from engineers or the general public', one journal reported at the time. [7]

At least four of Webb's engines were exhibited:

Marchioness of Stafford at the Inventions Exhibition, London, in 1885, where it won a gold medal; [1] Compound 2-2-4-0 Tank No. 777 at the Manchester Exhibition of 1887; *Jeanie Deans* at the Edinburgh Exhibition, 1890, where it won a gold medal; and *Queen Empress* at the Chicago World's Fair, 1893, where it too won a gold medal.

Webb was quite prepared to indulge in publicity 'stunts' of all kinds. He reported the record runs of 'Precedent' class engine No. 955 to the *Railroad Gazette* in the form of letters from *Charles Dickens* [2], he had an engine built in 25½ hours [3], and, as further proof of his ability to present locomotive engineering in a vivid manner, there is the well known photograph of an 0-8-0 locomotive standing behind its equivalent in raw materials. [4]

Webb's publicising talent did not only benefit the LNWR (and F. W. Webb). He quickly realised the excellence of David Joy's radial valve gear and worked for its recognition: 'Was down at Crewe, and showed Webb my plan. He immediately took to it, as he was designing a new type of big express goods engine, and this gear gave him very large bearings. In the Autumn we settled it, and he was at once to start an engine to exploit the plan, and then to allow it every possible publicity. I allowed LNWR a nominal royalty. Well, Webb did fairly fulfil his part of the bargain, and it was due to this that the plan was so soon and so prominently before the public.' [5]

The LNWR had gained another bargain. In exchange for Webb's encouragement – he provided a locomotive for the Barrow meeting of the Institution of Mechanical Engineers when Joy read a paper on his invention – the Company paid only 'nominal' royalties.

Having discussed various aspects of Webb's work, it is still necessary to explain why he had such a powerful position in the LNWR. The key would appear to be his appreciation that the governing factor in the Company's affairs was economy.

Professor Simmons suggests that this 'tradition of carefulness' (as he calls it) was inherited from the London & Birmingham Railway [6]. Certainly, under the chairmanship of Sir Richard Moon thrift was the first consideration: 'The Chairman's leading idea was "economy"; though sometimes strangely lavish in large matters he was almost penurious in others – his desire was to make the line a paying affair. In the part of London in which I resided, it was customary to supply the householders with cards having the letter "D" to place on the windows – this indicated that the Dustmen were

(1) F. A. S. Brown, *Nigel Gresley* (1961), p12.
(2) C. Hamilton Ellis, *Twenty Locomotive Men*, p193-4
(3) C. Hamilton Ellis, *British Railway History, 1877-1947*, p312.
(4) H. A. V. Bulleid, *Master Builders of Steam* (1963, p16-7).
(5) O. S. Nock, *Locomotives of the North Eastern Railway* (1954), p74.
(6) C. Hamilton Ellis, *The South Western Railway* (1956), p133.
(7) *Railway Engineer*, Vol 12 (1891), p309.

(1) There are two excellent photographs of the LNWR stand at the 1885 exhibition (BR LM Region negs DM 9008 and DM 9010). The stand is labelled 'LNWR: F. W. Webb's exhibit'.
(2) *Railroad Gazette* for 3.12.1886 and 2.10.1891.
(3) Chaloner, p73, and *Railroad Gazette*, Vol 20 (1888), p634-5.
(4) *Engineering*, Vol 64 (1897), p793-4: also *Railway Master Mechanic* for March 1898.
(5) *The Railway Magazine*, Vol 22 (1908) p319.
(6) Jack Simmons, *The Railways of Britain* (1961), p8.

required. On one occasion he told me he had observed these, and that he had always the letter "D" in his office window. To him it meant Dividend and he could not allow it to be lost sight of in any expenditure that was discussed.' [1]

Webb whole-heartedly supported this policy: the obituary notice in *The Locomotive Magazine* points out that he 'effected economies which, on the turnover of a huge organisation such as he controlled, can only be characterised as immense.' [2] The production and use of Bessemer steel and improved factory methods enabled him to make cheap engines: 'Early in his career at Crewe he claimed that he was building the cheapest locomotives in the world – excellence not being sacrificed. It was said that he turned out a single driver passenger engine, with cylinders 17in by 24in, and tender, for £1,800.' [3]

Ahrons says that Webb's 17in 0-6-0 coal engines 'were probably the simplest and cheapest locomotives ever made in this country,' [4] (elsewhere the figure is given as £400 [5]) and illustrates Webb's care by pointing out that he 'made the bearings of his goods engine ¹/₈in larger in diameter than those of his passenger engines, so that the axle-boxes of the latter, when worn, could be re-bored to suit the goods engines.' [6]

The whole episode of compounding was an attempt to reduce fuel costs, but Webb also ensured that nothing was wasted. Charlie Dick points out that 'from the scrap we make nails ... we make iron hurdles for fencing off the rails out of old rails and other scrap ...' [7] and Sams describes the economic use of wheel centres. [8] Acworth noted that LNWR notices were made up of individual raised letters (cast from scrap metal), which were screwed on the boards enabling them to be painted by 'any common labourer.' [9]

The economy drive on the LNWR did not go unnoticed. Acworth was told at the locomotive department of another company, 'We say here that the Crewe engines are made up of the best cast iron and the best lampblack.' [1] The decision, in April 1873, to paint the engines black, or more accurately Blackberry Black, produced a famous story. Webb was asked by a fellow member of the Institution of Civil Engineers why he painted his engines such a funereal colour, and he replied: 'Sir, when my shareholders are receiving 10 per cent on their money, I shall be pleased to cover my engines with gold leaf.' [2] It is interesting to realise that a gilded Webb locomotive can actually be seen – a model of the four-cylinder compound *King Edward VII* on the South African War Memorial in Queen's Park Crewe.

Economy is the final, sad note of Webb's career. In the minutes of the Board Meeting of 15th May 1903, appears this item:

'19153 Retirement of Mr F. W. Webb

It was agreed, in order to mark their sense of Mr Webb's devotion to the Company's interests during his long service, and their personal regard for him, that a sum of £1,000 be placed at the disposal of the Chairman, to be expended in such a manner as may be decided upon after consultation with Mr Webb.'

Nothing further is heard of this matter until the Board Meeting of 15th June 1906:

'21293 Retirement of Mr Webb ...

The Chairman reported the decease on the 4th June of Mr F. W. Webb and suggested that Minute 19153 should be rescinded, which was approved. It was agreed to defer for further consideration the question of what steps, if any, should be taken to mark the Board's appreciation of his long service to the Company.'

Sir Richard Moon and Webb were gone but the policy of economy continued.

(1) G. P. Neale, *Railway Reminiscences*, p126.
(2) *The Locomotive Magazine*, Vol 12 (1906), p88.
(3) *The Engineer*, Vol 101 (1906) p579.
(4) Ahrons, *BSRL*, p204.
(5) *LRCWR*, Vol 60 (1954), p4.
(6) Ahrons, *BSRL*, p226.
(7) Peter Taylor, *Autobiography* (1903), p185-6.
(8) *The Railway Magazine*, Vol 54 (1924), p384.
(9) W. M. Acworth, *The Railways of England*, p65.

(1) W. M. Acworth, *The Railways of England*, p62.
(2) This version of the story appears in Acworth's *The Railways of England*, p65; Steel, p351; *The Railway Magazine*, Vol 88 (1942), p329. What is probably the true account lies unread in *ICE*, Vol 81 (1885), p135: 'He had once been attacked by a member of the Shareholders' Audit Committee for painting the engines black. His reply was that when they paid 10 per cent, he would line them with gold.'

1b - Narrative of the search and compilation

The following is an account of the sources tried, the methods employed and the problems encountered during this study. It is hoped that it will provide a plan of approach for those making similar studies of the 'middle period' railway engineers.

Scope of the study
It is essential to define the scope of the study with some precision if unnecessary work is to be avoided. In every aspect of Webb's career there is a danger of widening the field to include marginal material. Unless this is kept in mind there is a tendency to cover the whole history of compounding instead of concentrating upon Webb's contribution, or to pay too much attention to the history of Crewe Works before and after Webb's period, or to start writing a general history of Crewe or the LNWR.

Strictly limiting the work to Webb's own developments leaves a large amount of material to be covered. Not only did he contribute to locomotive design and production methods, he also carried out important developments in the production and application of steel to rails, boilers, fireboxes, and so forth, and introduced his own ideas in signalling, rolling stock design, braking and many other fields. If these are to be adequately investigated there will be little time left for marginal research.

On the other hand, the study must be kept in perspective with the larger aspects of the subject, if false emphases are not to be laid. If Webb and the LNWR are considered in isolation, there is the possibility that they will gain too much importance and significance. There were other companies and other CMEs making their contributions to the development of British railways and the reader must be kept aware of this fact. Frequent re-reading of Hamilton Ellis's *British Railway History* will enable the researcher to keep his sense of balance.

This then is the problem of background information: how much is one to provide? A statement like 'Webb introduced 0-8-0 engines on the LNWR in 1892' has little significance unless it is related to other facts. Were there predecessors on other railways, or were these the first 0-8-0 engines ever built? Did they influence later LNWR locomotive policy or was it an isolated design? Did they influence locomotive design on other railways? These matters are relevant but there is still a danger of overloading the study with this kind of information so that the work of Webb is lost in general railway history.

Frequent decisions will have to be made and the scope of the study will have to be kept in mind, if the correct amount of background material is to be provided.

Selection of material
In the basic survey of sources and the compilation of the bibliography some selection, of a strictly limited kind, is necessary. Webb made a mass of information available to the editors of technical periodicals, and some of these news items, especially those giving running details of his compounds, seem to contribute very little. Such items have not been recorded, but the size of the item has not been the deciding factor, for short news paragraphs often contain more information than some full-length articles.

The need for selection is not limited to periodical articles. Most of the popular railway books, and many general locomotive engineering books, make reference to the work of Webb. To record all of these would be an unrewarding task. Occasionally, one of these general books is found to have remarkably good illustrations, as Charles S. Lake's *The World's Locomotives*, or to contain information that is not readily obtainable elsewhere, as W. M. Acworth's *The Railways of England*. In these cases entries have been made in the form of footnotes to essays or as bibliography entries.

The studies of the economics of railway transport have not been included. A study of Webb must assess him in terms of the economic stresses and demands of his time. These were the factors which determined LNWR policy and directed his work. The books of such scholars as C. E. R. Sherrington were consulted but, somewhat reluctantly, it was decided that they were too marginal for inclusion in the bibliography.

The vast literature, periodicals and books, of railway modelling has not been searched systematically. It was not thought that there would be sufficient new economic, social or engineering material to justify the work involved. There is much fringe material, however, that it would be a mistake to ignore. Examples include J. N. Maskelyne's two magnificent albums containing his drawings and personal reminiscences (*Locomotives I have known* and *A Further Selection of Locomotives I have known*) and F. C. Hambleton's *Locomotives Worth Modelling*. The latter contains useful detail drawings and the dimensions of a selection of Webb engines.

With reference to these three books another point must be mentioned. Every attempt has been made to reduce the amount of personal bias in the assessment of books mentioned in this study, but the fact remains that, despite one's attempts to be objective, many books have an appeal which is in terms of presentation and the author's personality, while the information content may not really justify inclusion in the bibliography.

Manuscript sources: letters and papers
The major sources for a study of this kind would normally take the form of letters, diaries, work-books and notes written by the subject. Unfortunately, a long search for the papers of F. W. Webb has proved fruitless.

The following collections were tried:

British Transport Commission Historical Records (now BRBHR)
Crewe Works

The British Museum (Department of Printed Books and Department of Manuscripts)
The Bodleian Library, Oxford
John Rylands Library, Manchester (including the Kenneth Brown Railway Collection)
The Science Museum
Crewe Public Library
Bournemouth Public Library
Liverpool Public Library
Manchester Public Library
Manchester University
National Register of Archives
Chester County Record Office
Hampshire County Record Office
Staffordshire County Record Office
Institution of Civil Engineers
Institution of Locomotive Engineers
Institution of Mechanical Engineers
Iron and Steel Institute
Stephenson Locomotive Society

A further attempt to locate letters and papers was made by appealing for information in a selection of periodicals. An item appeared in the 'Information, please' column of *The Times Literary Supplement* [1], an advertisement was inserted in *The Railway Magazine* [2], and letters were sent to the editors of *The Library Association Record* [3] and the two Crewe newspapers. *The Crewe Guardian* also printed a short news item and further appeal for information when the author made a second visit to Crewe. [4] Useful correspondences with G. Nulty, W. Pover and Neil Fraser arose out of these appeals but no new papers were found.

The following sources were tried for material concerning Stanway Manor, Webb's Shropshire home: Shrewsbury Public Libraries; Shropshire County Record Office; and Clerk to the Ludlow Rural District Council.

A visit was made to the estate, and the present owner, Major G. L. Y. Radcliffe, MBE, produced documents which show that Webb purchased the house and 550 acres of land in 1890 for £12,000. In 1905 Webb was proved to be 'in lunacy' and his brother, Canon Webb, was given powers to sell the estate.

Manuscript sources: company records

The minute books of the various LNWR committees are available at the BRB Historical Records. Some are of little interest: although Webb was in attendance at the Passenger Traffic Committee and the General Stores Committee, the minutes add little to our understanding of Webb's activities. The minutes of the Locomotive and Engineering Committee, in contrast, give a valuable insight into the daily work and responsibilities of the Chief Mechanical Engineer. The items concerning Webb fall roughly into five groups:

(1) Developments in the works. These include enlargement of shops, purchase of new plant, and similar matters. Examples are: the purchase of a 'plate edge planing machine' (February 1881); replacement of a 30 ton duplex hammer (April 1898); and completion of a new 2000 ton hydraulic press (February 1902).

(2) Such diverse things as gas and water supply (to Crewe and elsewhere), electricity installations, heating of Crewe schools, a new boiler for Euston Hotel (February 1897), sale of old engines and repayment for damage to property by fire from passing engines.

(3) Construction and installation of line apparatus – turn-tables, cranes, water columns, water troughs, signal apparatus, cabins, sheds and sidings and engine-men's lodging houses.

(4) Welfare of work people. Extension of hospitals, accident pay, re-instatement of defaulting employees, applications for artificial limbs, staff gratuities for special work, 'Running Department Mutual Insurance Society', 'Works Mutual Insurance Society', 'Locomotive Foremen's Pension Fund'. In some of these matters a remarkable amount of concern and consideration was shown; for example, in paying allowances to dependants in the South African War it was found 'more convenient to make these payments monthly and to the middle of each month as the Government Allowances are paid on the last day, so making the dependants some allowance every fortnight'. (January 1900).

(5) Mr Webb's monthly report to the committee includes some useful figures: numbers of engines under and awaiting repair (these figures were given to the January 1872 meeting when there were 325 engines under repair and 20 awaiting repair), production of rails, given in tons (example 1,818 in July 1879 and 3,743 tons in August 1896); and, latterly, the number of engine failures. Rather surprisingly, the number of engines constructed is not given.

Material at Crewe

A visit to Crewe emphasizes the need for urgency in research of this nature. Every year more material is lost and destroyed; every year old LNWR employees' memories die with them.

Many of the places associated with Webb have gone and others are changing. No.1 Chester Place, the official residence of the CME, has been demolished, and the Webb Orphanage has outlived its original usefulness. The eagles on Flag Lane Bridge [1] survive, however, although the bridge has been raised to allow electrification of the line, and the model of Webb's four-cylinder compound engine *King Edward VII* still adorns the War Memorial in Queen's Park.

An attempt was made to trace the portraits and busts to which reference is made in the *Dictionary of National Biography* article on Webb. One bust and one portrait (that by C. H. Charnock) remain at the Memorial Cottage Hospital. The bust is used as a door-stop and the portrait has been damaged. The Hall Neale portrait still hangs in the Orphanage Board Room.

The situation at Crewe Works is not very encouraging. The old records have recently been destroyed

(1) *The Times Literary Supplement*, Vol 62 (1963), p174
(2) *The Railway Magazine*, Vol 103 (1962), advert p vi in No. 740.
(3) *Library Association Record*, Vol 64 (1962), p494.
(4) *CG*, 18th July 1963, p8.

(1) Nock, *LNWR*, p58

(about 1960), apparently without consultation with the British Railways Archivist. Two slight, but interesting, records have survived. In the Paint Shop there is a slim ledger entitled 'Crewe Works: new engines painted from 1847'. This is a record of every engine passing through the Shop, and it gives such notes as 'first new engines painted black' (2nd November 1871), 'first iron number plates' (11th January 1873), and 'brass number plates' (as on 19th January 1877). Annual totals are given, the totals in Webb's reign being as follows:

1871	104	1877	108
1872	126	1878	75
1873	153	1879	92
1874	123	1880	106
1875	121	1881	88
1876	59	1882	91

This record was carelessly kept latterly and finally petered out in September 1884.

The other record is another, larger ledger kept as a press-cutting book in the General Offices. It consists mainly of cuttings taken from American periodicals (as *The Railroad Gazette* and *The Railway Age*) in the 1880s and 1890s. The blue pencil markings (used to indicate which column of the paper were to be preserved) may well be the work of Webb, while the inked dates and headings would be added by the clerk responsible for this book. It is possible here to see Webb's interests at this time. Many of the cuttings contain discussions of his system of compounding, and he must have been aware of the doubts and criticisms that are sometimes expressed in them.

Two important collections which are still to be found at the Works – the drawings and the photographic negatives – will be described in a later section of the thesis.

Anecdotal material

The stories that are handed down in railway families and in railway workshops are at once entertaining and unreliable. With each telling they become more exaggerated and embellished. Many of them have found their way into the popular railway literature of such capable and entertaining writers as O. S. Nock, Canon Roger Lloyd and Cuthbert Hamilton Ellis. There are many as yet unrecorded, however, and a number were collected for this study by Mr 'Bill' Pover, a fitter at Crewe Works. Although of limited value, they often contain the kind of information that could not be gathered elsewhere. There is, for example, the story that Webb courted Richard Moon's daughter. [1] This has lead at least one writer to suggest that Webb's cold and autocratic manner resulted from her refusal to marry him. Another story says that Webb also courted the daughter of Mr Thompson (co-patentee of a number of Webb's inventions). Mr Thompson is said to have disapproved of this match. [2]

Many of the stories illustrate the stern and exacting nature of Webb: Two pipe fitters were working on a stop valve near to the works and on finishing the job one said to the other, 'Well, I suppose that will do'. Unluckily for them, Mr Webb was within earshot and he came over and said in his usual stern tone: 'My man, either it is correct or it is not. There is no such thing as "I suppose that will do". Only the best will do, so take another look at your work.' [1]

Mr Dunn has given me a story which illustrates Webb's respect for craftsmanship and his interest in technical training: 'Webb took considerable interest in the education of the loco staff and, as one instance of this, he had a beautiful wooden model of the cylinders and motion of a 4-cylinder compound specially made at the request of the Bangor Loco. Improvement Class. This was done by one of the pattern-makers in the Works at Crewe, and when finished, he took it to Webb for his approval. F. W. W. said it was too good to go to a steam-shed – it was made in mahogany – and asked the pattern-maker to make another in deal for the shed. This he did, and was rewarded by promotion to Crewe Drawing Office.' [2]

Technical details can also be amusingly illustrated with such anecdotes as the following. The three-cylinder compounds of the 'Greater Britain' class were so long that in order to go on to the turn-tables they were close-coupled to the tender. This placed the hand-rails to the cab so close together that at least one corpulent driver could only get on and off the foot-plate when the train was on a curve.' [3]

Another story is associated with the Webb and Thompson frame, dated 1898, which is still in use at the time of writing (October 1963) in Gresty Lane No. 1 Box outside Crewe. There seems to be a ritual carried-out when a new man is introduced to this signal box. He is asked to set the road and if he tries to pull off before all the setting operations are completed, he is greeted with a chorus of, 'Now my lad, you can't do that. Mr Webb's got hold of you', from the other signal-men. He is then shown the correct procedure. [4]

There is a strong nostalgia in these stories. Although Webb was severe and uncompromising, he was a 'character'. Although he was powerful and important, he also made Crewe, the Works and his men important. One was proud to work at Crewe and one took pride in the work one did for the Company. Many a more liberal and more popular CME failed to create such a spirit or to leave such a legend.

Printed sources: bibliographies

Unfortunately there is no adequate bibliographical guide to railway literature. Professor Jack Simmons has provided a brief survey in his book *The Railways of Britain* [5] which, although limited in size, has the virtue

(1) C. Hamilton Ellis, *Twenty Locomotive Men*, p146 and elsewhere.
(2) Told to Mr Pover by Mr 'Charlie' Price (a long retired draughtsman living at 88 Church Lane, Wistaston, Crewe).

(1) *ibid.*
(2) Letter to the author dated 22.9.1963.
(3) Told to Mr Pover by Driver 'Tommy' Powell.
(4) Information supplied by Mr W. Pover and Mr G. Nulty.
(5) Section 8: Literature and maps, p233-50.

of being evaluative. In this survey we are informed that a comprehensive bibliography is being prepared by Mr George Ottley.

In the absence of a specialised work it is necessary to use such obvious sources as the British Museum Subject Catalogue, the London Library Catalogue and the Cumulative Book Index. It is clear that such important items as the pamphlets issued by the LNWR and the unions will not always be found in these works and it is thus necessary to see such catalogues as those issued by Mr Norman Kerr, the specialist in transport literature, from his book shop at Grange-over-Sands.

Printed sources: basic books

In a study of this kind a few books are found to be of constant use for providing basic information and for checking details: they form, in fact, a reference library on the subject

In this study five books were continually in use: Dr W. H. Chaloner's *The Social and Economic Development of Crewe, 1780-1923*, is a full and reliable history of the town and rarely failed to answer the queries that arose in this study. O. S. Nock's *The London and North Western Railway* provided a history of the company, and his *Premier Line* provided a history of the locomotives, with useful lists of numbers and names. H. F. F. Livesey's *The Locomotives of the LNWR* was found to be particularly useful as it is in the form of a chronology.

Few railway books could be written without incurring a great debt to E. L. Ahrons. His study, *The British Steam Railway Locomotive, 1825-1925*, was found to be essential for its engineering approach, especially for checking technical details. It is well illustrated and has an excellent index.

These books do not give all the information required, however, and the information given is not always in the form that is needed. It was therefore found necessary to compile three further aids:

1) A reference folder of locomotive classes, giving the basic technical details (number and diameter of wheels, cylinder diameter and stroke, heating surface, grate area, boiler pressure, etc), and the list of names and numbers. The is essential as, unfortunately, no book adequately establishes the various classes and their chronology. Only a compilation of this kind can solve the queries that arise due to lack of system in nomenclature. Sometimes a locomotive class is given the name of the first engine of the class, or by the nature of its work (Mineral, Goods, Passenger), sometimes by the diameter of the driving wheels and sometimes by the number of coupled wheels.

2) Another essential aid is a collection of locomotive photographs, arranged by class of engine. This can be used to clear up such minor points as variations in design (as the splashers on the classes of passenger compound engines) and even establish where specific locomotives were employed. Subsequently, choice of photographs for inclusion in the completed study can be made from this collection.

3) An outline or skeleton study consisting of notes made from the sources searched, roughly filed under topic or chapter headings. This enables variations of the same stories and technical data to be compared and permits more accurate evaluation of new material. It also reveals the difficulties of collection of information and shows where further research is necessary; for example, the scarcity of material on Webb's personal life was soon apparent.

Printed sources: periodicals

Periodical articles are a major source of information in a study of this kind, especially as Webb was a keen publicist and kept editors supplied with drawings, photographs, performance and other details of his new locomotives.

There are five groups of periodicals which must be searched:

(1) The newspapers. The Crewe newspapers are a major source of Webb's civic activities and they also contain some biographical material. The national newspapers, notably *The Times*, commented on the 'Intimidation Affair'.

(2) The transactions of the engineering institutions. Webb was an active member of the Institution of Civil Engineers, the Iron and Steel Institute and the Institution of Mechanical Engineers. As he read a number of papers, frequently took part in the discussions, and as his work was often the subject of comment by other speakers, these transactions are a major source.

Papers on compounding have also been read before the Institution of Locomotive Engineers, but this body was founded in 1911, long after Webb's time.

(3) The engineering magazines like *The Engineer*, *Engineering*, and *Railway Engineer*. Foreign periodicals (Continental and American) of this type are valuable as they often describe processes which, being standard practice in Britain, are overlooked in English periodicals.

(4) More general periodicals likely to contain contemporary accounts of the LNWR and Crewe activities, such as *Punch* and *Illustrated London News*.

Further periodicals will be traced from footnotes and other references and from such lists as *Willing's Press Guide*, *Ulrich's Periodicals Directory*, *BUCOP*, *World List of Scientific Periodicals Published ... 1900-1950*, H. C. Bolton's *Catalogue of Scientific and Technical Periodicals, 1665-1895*, the Science Museum Library *Hand List of Short Titles of Current Periodicals*, and the similar list of Patent Office holdings. Few of these are subject classified or indexed and reference has to be made under such key words as RAILWAY and LOCOMOTIVE.

Having selected the periodicals to be searched it is necessary to find a library where long runs of them are readily available. Most libraries have the early volumes of their periodicals in storage, often in distant buildings, so that notice (perhaps of a number of days) has to be given. This situation exists in the two most obvious sources of this type of material, the Science Museum Library and the Patent Office Library.

The searcher wishing to examine a long run of a periodical, and not merely to follow up a specific reference, finds that he is going to cause a great deal of trouble and that his search is going to be governed, perhaps, by the number of books that can be transported at one time.

An exception to this is the British Railways Board Historical Records Department (66 Porchester Road, London, W2) which has good holdings of many periodicals (*ICE, IMechE, The Engineer, Engineering, Railway Magazine*, etc) and has them readily available on shelves to which the reader has access. This is exemplary service to the researcher and it is unfortunate that the larger collections cannot provide similar facilities.

Periodical indexes

Adequate searching of periodicals is dependent upon the quality of the published indexes. Unfortunately, most indexes were found to be unreliable and left the searcher wondering if, in fact, he had managed to find all the relevant articles.

The Railway Magazine indexes have peculiarities but most of them can be mastered. After the groupings of 1923 LNWR items are indexed under LMS without cross-references. Some items only appear under HISTORICAL. The Webb interview of 1900, however, does not appear in the index under WEBB.[1] The indexes of the *Journal of the Stephenson Locomotive Society* are even more peculiar. The article 'Some Notes on F. W. Webb's Engines' is not indexed under LOCOMOTIVE INFORMATION but under GENERAL ITEMS, which is strictly correct in view of the contents of the article, but it is arranged under F – 'F. W. Webb's Engines, some notes on'. An article on Crewe Works is alphabetised at H – 'History of Crewe Locomotive Works'.

The technique employed in searching these indexes was to compile a list of topics likely to be found in the index, as:

> COMPOUNDING
> CREWE
> LOCOMOTIVES
> LNWR
> WEBB

This ensured that all the possible headings were searched. In some cases new headings, peculiar to the index, were found and the list was altered and some indexes were scanned for a second time. The final list for searching *The Railway Magazine* was

> CREWE
> HISTORICAL
> LOCOMOTIVES
> LMS – in later vols.
> LNWR
> WEBB

In order to ensure that all volumes were searched a volume list was typed out and this was ticked as the volumes were seen, thus:

> 1 v
> 2 v
> 3 v
> 4 ---x not seen
> 5 v
> 6

This was particularly useful when incomplete files were consulted (as the *Railway Magazine* at Swindon Public Library) as the missing volumes were noted and could be consulted elsewhere.

Entries for periodical articles were transferred to 5in by 3in cards in this form:

> *Railway Magazine*, Vol 8 (1901), p360-6
> LAKE, Charles S.
> The express locomotives of a great railway.
> [ie LNWR]

Annotations were added to define the scope of the article and to evaluate it in terms of information content and illustrative materials. Separate entries were made for obituaries and portraits.

The following is a check list of the periodicals searched:

Cassier's Magazine	Vol 7-26 (1895-1904).
Crewe Chronicle	Vol for 1890, 1900, 1901, 1903,1906.
Crewe Guardian	Vol for 1871, 1887-1890, 1903, 1906.
Eardley's Crewe Almanack	Vol for 1873, 1875, 1878, 1883, 1885, 1887-1905,1907.
Engineer	Vol 31-96, 101 (1871-1903, 1906)
Engineering	Vol 10-82 (1870-1906)
Fielden's Magazine	Vol 1-9 (1899-1903)
Locomotive, Railway Carriage and Wagon Review (1896-1959. 1896 Vol called *Moore's Monthly Magazine*, later volumes until 1921 called *Locomotive Magazine*). All seen.	
North-Western Locomotive Journal Vol 1-2 (1899)	
Punch	Vol for 1873-9, 1880-2, 1888, 1895.
Railroad Gazette	Vol 19-35 (1887-1903) (Vol 38 (1906) checked by American correspondent for obituary notice).
Railway Digest	Vol 1-4 (1947-50).
Railway Engineer	Vol 1-24, 27 (1880-1903,1906).
Railway Magazine	All checked to date.
Railway World	All checked to date.
(until 1953 called *Railways*).	
Trains Illustrated	All checked to Vol 15 (1962).

Also Journals, Proceedings, etc of the following bodies:
> Institution of Civil Engineers
> Institution of Locomotive Engineers
> Institution of Mechanical Engineers
> Iron and Steel Institute
> Railway and Canal Historical Society
> Stephenson Locomotive Society
> (*Journal* Vol 32-37(1956-61) searched).

[1] *Railway Magazine*, Vol 6 (1900), p97-107. Fortunately, *Railway Magazine* has been independently indexed at the BRBHR.

Organisation of the material

There are two problems here. The first is to arrange the bibliography so that it provides a survey of the available material on the various aspects of Webb's life and work. The second is the arrangement of the material in the correct sequence for the finished study.

The arrangement of the bibliography is, to some extent, a mechanical process. It is necessary to have a flexible outline scheme but the material itself will dictate what subdividing is required. For example, entries on Webb's inventions will either (a) be so few that they can remain under a general heading or (b) become so numerous that sub-headings are essential. Where there is a choice of a number of arrangements – alphabetically by author or topic, chronologically by date of writing or period discussed – the governing factor is, obviously, that of usefulness. Which arrangement will reveal the most information? For example, there was a choice of three arrangements of the material on the locomotives:

(1) Strictly chronological arrangement by the date that the first engine of each class was built. This system would reveal most about Webb's general design development and the traffic needs of the company, but it would separate similar classes of engine and mingle simple with compound locomotives.

(2) Chronological arrangement within broad group headings – passenger, goods, etc. This would be difficult as there were a number of mixed-traffic engines, but the value of arranging the engines by the type of work for which they were built has obvious usefulness.

(3) Division into simple and compound engines and then sub-division by class and finally by date. This would bring the material on the controversial compounds together.

The first arrangement was finally selected but as can be seen each of the possible schemes had much in its favour. No arrangement can serve all the possible purposes of the bibliography.

The arrangement of material for the final study is a more complex matter. It will depend upon such factors as the amount of information available, the approach which the writer wishes to make (biographical, economic, engineering, etc), the probable requirements of the readership to which he is directing the study, and his own qualifications and inclinations.

Biographical material

Despite Professor Simmons' warning that 'the great *Dictionary of National Biography* deals most inadequately with railwaymen, as with engineers and entrepreneurs of all kinds' [1], in fact, the entry on Webb by William Forbes Spear [2] provides an adequate basis for the biographical aspect of this study. (Although Webb did not appear in *Who's Who*, his brother, Col Walter George Webb, was given an entry. [3])

(1) Jack Simmons, *The Railways of Britain*, p242.
(2) *Dictionary of National Biography: supplement*, January 1901 - December 1911, p623-5.
(3) *Who was Who*, 1916-1928, p1103-4.

Many of the stories about Webb are to be found in the popular railway books but the total picture obtained from these sources is, at best, a vague and lifeless thing. It is a mere mask, as unrevealing as the photographic portraits of Webb. Nowhere is there an indication of how Webb worked or lived, of his childhood and youth at Tixall, his education and training, his friendships and pastimes. Similarly, assessment of his character has been reduced to repetition of the words 'cold' and 'autocratic'.

It might be thought that the absence of personal papers and the destruction of official papers preclude the discovery of new material. Mr J. M. Dunn has shown that this is not so. In his research for his articles on Webb in the *Railway Magazine* he attempted to trace Webb's genealogy in order to find 'a reason for Webb junior's unaccountable rapid advancement on the LNWR and the Chairman, Richard Moon's continuous staunch support.' [1]

The following sources were tried:

1) The Episcopal Registers of the Diocesan Registry, Lichfield. These record the induction of Webb's father as vicar of Tixall, but there is no hint of his previous preferments. (Crockford's *Clerical Directory* first appeared in 1858 and so cannot help in this case).

Liber 29, p216.

TIXALL R. 15th July 1831.
WILLIAM WEBB Clerk Bachelor of Arts was instituted to the Rectory of Tixall in the County of Stafford and Diocese of Litchfield and Coventry void by the resignation of Thomas Walker Clerk the last incumbent on the presentations of George Keen of Rowley in the Parish of Castlechurch in the said County of Stafford Esquire true Patron (for this turn only) and a Mandate was issued to the Archdeacon of Stafford to induct him.

2) The Superintendent Registrar of Stafford. He was asked to trace the marriage of William Webb and Maria Morgan but reported that registration services did not begin until 1837. There were two churches where the marriage might have taken place, so Mr Dunn wrote to the vicar at each of them.

3) St Mary's Church, Stafford. There was no trace of the marriage in the registers.

4) Castle Church, Stafford. No reply was received to Mr Dunn's enquiry.

5) The vicar at Tixall was unable to find any record of the birth of Webb but reported that he was baptised in Tixall Church on 22nd May, 1836. 'Unless F. W. W. slept in what is our spare room', added the Vicar, 'he must have been able to watch the trains go past from his bedroom window.'

6) The census return for 1851 (Public Record Office H. O. 107/1999. Bk.3. E.D.1 pages 12 and 13). This pro-

(1) Letter from Mr Dunn to Lichfield Diocesan Registrar, 15th June 1960.

vides the birthplaces of the parents and also establishes that Francis W. was educated at home.

During this search, Mr Dunn's attention was drawn to an item in a minute, dated 11th November 1856, of the LNWR Northern Division Sub-Committee (LNW 1/163, p261):

'Mr Trevithick reported that Frank Webb, draughtsman in his office, is out of his apprenticeship and that he is an exceedingly respectable young man and his services are very valuable.
Resolved that it be a recommendation to the Executive Committee to retain Webb's services at £2-0-0 a week wage.'

This provides the clue to Webb's advancement and also supports Michael Robbins' claim that a characteristic of the railway career was 'that it owed nothing to any influence except the man's own work and the impression that it made on his superiors.' [1]

In addition to Mr Dunn's finds my attention has been drawn to an entry in *Alumni Cantabrigiensis*:
Webb, William. Adm. Pens. (age 18) at Trinity, 1 July 1824. Son of Henry. Born at Castle Church, Staffs. Rector of Tixall 1831-83. Died 27 March 1883. Father of Arthur H. (1853) and William J. (1863).

A search of the Crewe newspapers reveals much detail about Webb's early life and interests which has not found its way into the books. For example, when the Freedom of Crewe was conferred upon Webb in June, 1900, Councillor A. G. Hill gave some examples of the early emergence of his practical nature. As a child he made a wheelbarrow:
'He was so pleased with it that in 1847 he became rather more ambitious, and then built a pony cart. When that was completed there was great joy in the village of Tixall, and the cart was exhibited on the village green, much to the admiration of the inhabitants'. [2] (Pride in exhibiting his products never left Webb. In later years he was to display his locomotives whenever the opportunity arose).

'About that time the parish church was being restored, and it was his delight to get among the masons and try his hand at any kind of work. In fact, several parts of the church were finished by him, and some figures were sculptured entirely by himself ... Further than that, in his early days he showed his aptitude by taking contracts: he believed that he built a garden wall at 3d per yard ... Not content with that, he assisted in the decoration of a house.' [3]

In his Mayoral address in 1886, Webb described his early days at Crewe, when he was a pupil of Francis Trevithick. He lodged with the barber, Richard Sherwin, who had a shop at the corner of Mill Street: 'Those were happy days. I had no weight of responsibility. I got out of the Works and on to the cricket field, and that reminds me that I was connected with the first cricket club that was started at Crewe ... The roller now in the possession of Crewe Club is one I moulded with my own hands. It was not a foreign order though – (loud laughter) – as I had permission to make it, and was as proud of that bit of work, when I turned it out, as I am of the finest locomotives that Crewe Works can produce'. [1]

At the twenty-first dinner of the Crewe Cricket Club in 1871 Webb noted that he was 'one of the oldest members having joined it at its commencement, 21 years ago.' [2]

Elsewhere he is spoken of as the founder of the Club. [3] According to Dr Atkinson, speaking at the opening of the Alexandra Athletic Ground in May 1898:
'Nine young men met together [in 1850] and each put down 1s 6d, which in those days was regarded as a large sum. With this money they bought a pair of bats and two balls.' [4]

The speaker goes on to describe how permission was granted by Trevithick to have stumps and bails turned in the Works. One wonders if the young Webb was the chosen spokesman for the new club.

Cricket was not the only pastime that Webb enjoyed. He was also a keen gardener and was for may years the Vice President of the Crewe and District Chrysanthemum Society and the Crewe Horticultural Society. On at least one occasion his exhibits – '(gardener J.Smith)' – won prizes at the Crewe Flower Show. [5]

One practical result of his love of plants was divulged at the visit of the British Association to Crewe in 1887: 'A few years after he came to Crewe the place was becoming a second Sheffield for smoke; but he was fond of plants ... Having to live in Crewe, and wishing to encourage the growth of plants, he felt it his duty to clear the atmosphere as much as possible, and when they [the members of the British Association] went round the works they would see that they had almost done away with the smoke ... He thought if some of the members of the Association took up the question of smoke nuisance and how to avoid it ... large towns like Manchester and Liverpool could be almost cleared of it.' [6] (It would be interesting to know how many other people were concerned about smoke abatement at the time).

Apart from these interests W. H. Acworth notes in an article in *Murray's Magazine*: 'He [Webb] devotes his leisure to agriculture, and speaks on the subject before the Cheshire Agricultural Society, of which he was the president for the year 1887.' [7]

In addition to these positions, Webb was for many years president of the Crewe Philharmonic Society, Crewe Mechanics' Institute Chess and Draughts Club,

(1) Michael Robbins, *The Railway Age*, (1962), p93.
(2) *CG*, 20th June 1900, p5.
(3) *CG*, 23rd June 1900, p5.

(1) Quoted *CG*, 4th May 1934, p7.
(2) *CG*, 11th November 1871, p5.
(3) *CG*, 22nd May 1936, p9.
(4) Quoted *CG*, 9th July 1926, p7.
(5) *CG*, 14th August 1886, p
(6) *CG*, 10th September 1887, p4.
(7) Quoted *CG*, 28th December 1887, p3.
Correspondence with the Cheshire Agricultural Society has failed to produce any further information.

the Crewe Britannia Bowling Club and the Crewe Shorthand Writers' Association. His personal interest in some of these societies is open to doubt, but the same cannot be said of two other bodies for which he acted as president. He actively supported the Crewe Mechanics' Institute, not interfering with its management but rarely missing the annual meeting and the prize giving, and he took similar interest in the Crewe Scientific Society to which reference has already been made.[1]

Some new material is slight. A curious hint of Webb's character, for example, is provided by the device on his personal letter headings. This consists of a monogram embossed in blue in the form of a large F from the top line of which depend two small w's. The lower part of the F contains a spider on a web. There is something at once rather childish and sinister about this device.

Webb is always described as a friendless man but the will of 'Francis Wm. Webb Esquire of Chester Place Crewe and Stanway Manor Salop' reveals that this was not so.[2] It lists some of his friends: Dr James Atkinson (the company surgeon at Crewe) and George Robert Jebb (a Birmingham engineer), who are described in the *Crewe Guardian* obituary as 'two life-long friends', and Arther Griffiths Hill (his solicitor). To Charles Mason (a Wolverton engineer) was left his 'pair of guns rifle cartridge magazine and fittings' which Webb, no doubt, had used on his grouse shooting days in Scotland. The newspaper accounts of the funeral note that most of these friends were present. It is interesting to note, however, that George Whale, his successor, did not attend the funeral: he was represented by the Works Manager, Mr A. R. Trevithick. The *Crewe Chronicle* notes that there was a wreath from 'the Hon. R. B. C. Scarlett, an old pupil.' It would be interesting to know the cause of this devotion.

The 'lost years': 1866-1871

Every biography seems to include a black period when there is little knowledge of the subject's activities. In the case of Webb this period covers the years 1866 to 1871. During this time Webb was Works Manager of the Bolton Iron & Steel Company. Considering the facts that the Librarian of Bolton has been able to find, it is unlikely that we will ever have any details of these years. The facts are these:

'The engineering works originated about 1830 by a William Platt. Upon his death, in 1835, his trustees became the proprietors.

In 1860 the undertaking was carried on by Messrs Hick, Hargreaves & Sharp as the Bolton Iron & Steel Company.

On 6th November 1906, it was announced that the entire undertaking of the Bolton Iron & Steel Company had been taken over by Henry Bessemer & Co Ltd of Sheffield.

(1) A complete account of these activities can be compiled from *Eardley's Crewe Almanack*.
(2) There is a copy of the will in the BRBHR.

On 17th March 1924, the directors announced the gradual closure of the Bolton Works, and in July 1924 the entire plant, etc, was sold, and in 1927 the site was cleared and bought by this Corporation. The site is in use for market and a bus station [sic].' [1] No business records of the Company can be traced.

In the summer of 1871, before succeeding Ramsbottom as the CME of the LNWR, Webb went on a tour of the railroads of the United States. In the hope of tracing an account of this visit, the following American libraries were approached:
Altoona Public Library.
Association of American Railroads, Washington.
Bureau of Railway Economics Library
Pennsylvania Railroad Company Library,
                    Philadelphia.
Rutherford B. Hayes Library, Fremont, Ohio.
None of these libraries was able to discover any account of the visit in either the local press or the railway magazines. It would be interesting to have Webb's impressions of the great Altoona Works of the Pennsylvania Railway Company, which might be described as the American Crewe, but it appears that they went unrecorded.

Medical history and retirement

Enquiry into the health, and particularly the mental health, of Webb is a piece of research that can give no pleasure, but it is essential as it provides a clue to his personality and explains the circumstances of his retirement.

There appears to have been a history of mental illness in the family. It is said that his sister, Mary, had to enter a mental institution and there is mention, in Webb's obituaries, of a life-long fear of mental illness. The obituary in *The Engineer* says that 'a fear of the disease to which in the end he succumbed overshadowed his life' [2] and that in *The Railway Times* suggests that this 'fear of break-down' made him the cold and distant man that he was.[3]

In 1902 there was an outbreak of false reports that Webb was retiring. A news item in *The Engineer* refuted these reports [4], as did *The Railway Engineer,* which noted that the false announcement had been made 'for about the sixth time.' [5] In July of the following year *The Railway Engineer* reported that 'Mr F. W. Webb's health has failed him to such an extent that he has been obliged to hand over the onerous duties ... to his appointed successor ... somewhat sooner than was arranged.' [6]

Whale's version of Webb's retirement is told in H. A. V. Bulleid's recent book: 'Webb was shown a new draw-

(1) Letter to the author dated 8th January 1963.
(2) *Engineer*, Vol 101 (1906, p579
(3) *Railway Times*, Vol 89 (1906), p731
(4) *Engineer*, Vol 94 (1902), p182
(5) *Railway Engineer*, Vol 23 (1902), p257
(6) *Railway Engineer*, Vol 24 (1903), p205

ing, to which he took an immediate dislike. He scribbled over it with a pencil held in his fist, tore it up, flung the pieces on to the floor and stamped on them. Too many of the staff witnessed this unfortunate scene. Whale, with the support of Trevithick and Bowen Cooke, went to Euston and reported to the Board that things could go on no longer in this way. Accordingly, Webb's retirement, already announced, was fixed definitely; and Whale took over on 1st May, 1903.' [1]

Webb's collapse seems to have been sudden. Until mid 1903 his programme was a full one. In February, for example, apart from his railway duties, he presided at the annual meetings of the Cottage Hospital and the Mechanics' Institute, and also opened the Exhibition of Arts and Crafts in the Town Hall. In April he opened the new physical laboratory at the Mechanics' Institute.

He seemed to have accepted the fact of his approaching retirement and had been sorting out his possessions. Some of these he had sent to his Church Stretton home and others, including 145 engineering books and engravings of the two Stephensons and of George Parker Bidder, he had given to the Mechanics' Institute. [2]

In the late news on the 30th May, *The Crewe Chronicle* reported 'that Mr F. W. Webb, who was taken ill some days ago and ordered away for complete change and rest, is lying at Colwyn Bay in a serious condition, and ... grave anxiety is felt concerning him.' [3] There was a news item in June saying that he had gone to a convalescent home in Staffordshire. [4] There were no further reports.

(1) H. A. V. Bulleid, *Master Builders of Steam*, p160-1.
(2) CC, 30th May 1903, p8.
(3) *ibid.*
(4) CC, 13th June 1903, p8.

Webb retired finally to The Red Lodge, Parsonage Road, Bournemouth, where he spent much of his time playing with toy trains and suffering from the delusion that he would end his days begging for bread on Crewe Station. [1] He died on 4th June 1906, leaving £75,000, of which five hundred pounds were left to the Royal Albert Asylum for Idiots and Imbeciles at Lancaster. The death certificate, unfortunately, does not mention Webb's mental condition but merely records the immediate cause of death as 'malignant disease of the peritoneum, 6 months'.

It will be necessary to have more evidence, and to have substantiation of existing evidence, if we are to arrive at the psychology of Webb, if we are to have the key to his attitudes and behaviour. Unfortunately, it is difficult to imagine what records might exist to supply any new material. As Hamilton Ellis has said: 'Just what ticked in the heart of this cold, bitter man none can tell now.' [2]

Further research
Although an attempt has been made in this study to pursue every possible line of enquiry, it is probable that more material lies hidden somewhere. There is still much work to be done and much to be discovered and explained.

In September 1962 the London & North Western Railway Historical Society was formed, its aim being 'to record all historical aspects of the company's activities.' [3] Perhaps this body will succeed in bringing further material to light.

(1) Information given by Dr W. H. Chaloner in a letter to the author dated 9th April 1963.
(2) Hamilton Ellis, *Twenty Locomotive Men*, p147.
(3) *Railway World*, Vol 24 (1963), p80.

2a - Biographical material

Books

Chaloner, W. H.
The Social and Economic Development of Crewe, 1780-1923, Manchester University Press, 1950. Well indexed. Many references to the local news papers *Crewe Chronicle* and *Crewe Guardian*. A most valuable source for many aspects of Webb's life, especially his local government affairs.

Dictionary of National Biography
Supplement, January 1901 – December 1911. This contains (p623-5) a good summary of Webb's life and career by William Forbes Spear.

Ellis, C. Hamilton
British Railway History,
Allen and Unwin, 2 Vol, 1954-9.
Well indexed. Mr Hamilton Ellis always takes a crit-ical view of Webb, even his title of CME (instead of locomotive superintendent) is remarked upon [1], and elsewhere we are told that his chimneys are 'puritanical-looking' [2] and his cabs 'paltry'. [3] Webb has a hard judge in Mr Hamilton Ellis.

Ellis, C.Hamilton
The Trains We Loved, Allen and Unwin, 1947.
A little more of 'the legend'.

Ellis, C. Hamilton.
Twenty Locomotive Men, Ian Allan, 1958.
Chapter 14 is one of the few attempts to assess Webb. The author raises the interesting theory that Webb may have spent his five years at the Bolton Iron & Steel Company because 'with so assured a future before him at Crewe he was found by Ramsbottom to be getting too imperious' (p136). The original text of this article appears in *LRCWR*, Vol 45 (1939), p179-82.

Lloyd, Roger.
Railwaymen's Gallery, Allen and Unwin, 1953.
Webb is the villain of this piece, p113-17, which seems to be mainly derived from Chaloner. Canon Lloyd does ask the interesting question why Sir Richard Moon permitted Webb such a degree of autonomy, a question that I have tried to answer in the opening essay.

Nock, O. S.
British Trains Past and Present, Batsford, 1951.
More fragments of 'the legend'.

(1) C.Hamilton Ellis, *British Railway History,* Vol 1, p411.
(2) C.Hamilton Ellis, *Some Classic Locomotives* (1949), p19.
(3) C.Hamilton Ellis, *The South Western Railway,* p97.

Nock, O. S.
The London and North Western Railway
Ian Allan, 1960.
Outlines 'the general policy of North Western loco motive practice' and supplements the next item.

Nock, O. S.
The Premier Line: the story of the London and North Western locomotives, Ian Allan, 1952.
Three chapters (6, 7 and 8) review Webb's work.

Nock, O. S.
Steam Locomotive, Allen and Unwin, 1957.
Some more fragments of 'the legend', including the story of the request to exhibit an engine at Edinburgh in 1890 (p72-3).

Steel, Wilfred L.
The History of the London and North Western Railway, Railway and Travel Monthly, 1914.
A disappointing book derived almost entirely from Sir George Findlay's *Working and Management of an English Railway* and G. P. Neale's *Railway Reminiscences*. Webb is dismissed (p459-67) with little more than a summary of his locomotive designs. There is nothing new and there is no attempt to assess Webb's career.

Periodical articles

Cassier's Magazine, Vol 10 (1896), p133-4.
Jackson, J. N.
'Francis William Webb, MInstCE, locomotive superintendent of the LNWR'
Nothing much here, except the Llandulas viaduct story.

LRCWR, Vol 45 (1939), p179-82.
Ellis, C. Hamilton.
'Famous locomotive engineers: 11. Francis William Webb'

Railroad Gazette, Vol 35 (1903), p422-3
Rous-Marten, Charles.
'The retirement of Mr F. W. Webb'
A useful summary of Webb's career with mention of his visit to America and the influence of American methods.

Railway Magazine, Vol 6 (1900), pp.97-107.
Illustrated interviews: No. 31, Mr Francis William Webb, MIME
Webb's character comes through in the opening words: 'I have a great disinclination ... to being made the subject of an interview, but I will make an exception in the present instance. You must, however, please be as brief as you can, for I am a busy man, as you know.'

The body of the interview is the routine Crewe 'publicity handout'.

Railway Magazine, Vol 54 (1924), p271-6, 382-6.
Sams, J. G. B.
'Recollections of Crewe', 1897-1902.
An account is given, p383, of Mr Sams' only encounter with Webb. It is a fleeting glimpse of Webb touring workshops.

Railway Magazine, Vol 88 (1942), p159-64.
Lake, Charles S.
'Some CMEs I have known: F. W. Webb'
Little material here.

Railway Magazine, Vol 107 (1961), p756-62, 840-4
Dunn, J. M.
'F. W. Webb, Crewe'
The latest, fullest and fairest assessment of Webb.

Obituary notices
Bournemouth Graphic, 14th June 1906.

Bournemouth Observer and Chronicle, 9th June 1906.
Text as in above. Little of interest except the list of mourners.

Crewe Chronicle, 9th June 1906 p5 (Editorial, p8)
A full (three and a half columns) obituary, particularly interesting as this is a Liberal paper that was in conflict with Webb.

Crewe Guardian, 9th June 1906, p 4-5.
A full (two and a quarter columns) obituary, including an account of the tributes to Webb given at the Town Council meeting.

Engineer, Vol 101 (1906), p579.
An important assessment of his character and career. 'A distinguishing feature of Mr Webb's character was intense faith in himself, very largely justified by the successes which he not infrequently secured'.
'Mr. Webb's temperament was peculiar, and he was not fortunate enough to make many friends. He never married, and there is little doubt that a fear of the disease to which in the end he suc cumbed overshadowed his life'.

Engineering, Vol 81 (1906), p764-5.

ICE, Vol 167, p373.
A cautious obituary notice.

ISI, 1906, i, p274-5.
Short, formal obituary.

Locomotive Magazine, Vol 12 (1906), p88.
Brief summary of Webb's career.

Railway Engineer, Vol 27 (1906), p201 and 237.
A remarkably full, informative and sympathetic notice.
Page 237 consists of details of the will.

Railway News, Vol 85 (1906), p1038.

Railway Times, Vol 89 (1906), p731.
An interesting and sympathetic obituary, indeed the warmest of them all.
'He had a host of admirers who would only too willingly have been admitted to closer acquaintance'.
'He brought [compound engines] to such perfection that they were introduced in France, in Austria, in India and in several of the South American States.' (This is charity at its most excessive).
'Mr Webb had the Napoleonic character which he shared with I. K. Brunel – no one of the three would delegate his authority to any, and they all wore themselves away by too close an attention to details – also they were all very self-willed and brooked no opposition'.
'He was a fine example of a masterly Englishman'.

The Times, 6th June 1906, p5.
Non-committal, indeed interesting for its evasion of any mention of Webb's character.

2b - F. W. Webb as inventor and member of the engineering institutions

'A large proportion of the new details introduced or tried
during this period [1876-1881] were due to F. W. Webb, who
was a veritable mechanical genius in respect of bold designs'.
E. L. Ahrons, (*BSRL*, p225)

Webb had the inventive genius and engineering imagination that is associated with the railway pioneers. No doubt this was, in part, due to the Crewe tradition. The first Locomotive Superintendent there was Francis Trevithick, son of Richard ('Father of the Locomotive Engine') and followed by John Ramsbottom who invented, among other things, the water pick-up apparatus, screw-reversing gear, the displacement lubricator, the double-beat regulator valve, the Ramsbottom safety valve and split piston rings.

During his life-time Webb patented eighty inventions, most of which were concerned with railways. Indeed, *The Times*' obituary noted that 'his inventions in connexion with railway plant are of themselves sufficient to fill a small museum.' [1] Although there is a suggestion here that the museum is the best place for them, some of the inventions had that simplicity which is the mark of genius: his casing for the Ramsbottom safety valve is an example.

It must be admitted, however, that, in this age of technological refinement, some of his inventions call to mind Lewis Carroll's White Knight. Such ideas, as the combustion chamber in his long boilers and his 'wet-bottom' firebox, seem impractical. Other inventions seem to be before their times: his patent buffer, for example, which is described by Acworth: 'If a train runs into what railway men term a "dead end", the injury is usually caused, not by the first shock, but by the subsequent recoil. To meet this, these buffers are designed, which press not against springs, as is ordinarily the case, but against a column of soapy water stored in a cylinder under huge pressure. A shock which forces back the buffers drives that water through minute holes into an outer jacket, and thence into an air-vessel under pressure, and there is then nothing left to cause them to spring back as the pressure of the blow gradually relaxes.' [2]

Another Webb experiment which suffered because it was before its time was the double chimney. In 1897 three engines were fitted with double blastpipe and chimney, the rebuilt Newton *Hampden* (No. 1542) and the four-cylinder compounds *Jubilee* and *Black Prince*. Pettigrew has described the arrangement: 'In the four-cylinder engines recently designed by Mr Webb, two blast pipes are employed with the object of obtaining a uniform distribution of draught over the tubes. The smokebox is divided by a horizontal partition into two compartments and a blast pipe is placed in each. Each compartment is provided with a separate chimney, that of the lower one passing through the upper.' [1]

Little advantage was obtained, however, and the idea was abandoned. That it was potentially a sound idea has been proved by later adoption of the double chimney on such classes as the GWR 'Castles'.

There is a curious inconsistency between Webb's whole-hearted adoption of compounding and his distrust of coupled driving wheels. In his three-cylinder compounds he left the two pairs of drivers uncoupled, his aim being 'to combine the flexibility of the single-driving engine with the increased power of the coupled engine.' [2] Then, in 1892, he tried to get the best of both worlds with his friction wheel: 'Upon the original No. 757 *Banshee* being withdrawn from service in 1892, Mr Webb fitted her experimentally with a friction wheel device in place of the usual coupling rods which were removed. The object was to combine the freedom of a single-driving wheel with the increased adhesion of coupled wheels. When required, the friction wheels on each side were raised by a mechanical arrangement into contact with both of the large wheels so as to transmit power from the driving wheels to those which, ordinarily, would be coupled therewith. At other times the trailing wheels ran as carriers only.' [3]

The friction wheel was abandoned, and with the 'Jubilee' class, built 1897 to 1900, came the return of coupled driving wheels on the LNWR.

Webb had a similar distrust of the bogie and used his double radial truck to carry the leading wheels of his 4-4-0s and 4-6-0s. Bowen Cooke explains that 'this truck has four wheels, but instead of being pivoted (as with the ordinary bogie), it is fitted with Mr Webb's radial axle-box, with central side-controlling spring.[4]

---

(1) W. F. Pettigrew. *A Manual of Locomotive Engineering*, (3rd ed, 1909), p228: note also a reference in *Railway Magazine*, Vol 8 (1901), p360-6, which includes a photograph of *Hampden* with the double chimney and a note that 'this innovation is still in the experimental stage'. Ahrons, *BSRL*, p310, notes that Webb abandoned the double chimney 'after about two years' service'.
(2) *The Times*, 6th June 1906, p5: Tuplin (*North Western Steam*, p70) suggests that Webb abandoned coupling rods because Joy valve-gear was too wide to leave room for them.
(3) *Railway Magazine*, Vol 44 (1919), p47. Note also Vol 18 (1906), p132-3, and an excellent photograph of *Banshee* fitted with the friction wheel (BR LM region, negative DM 9017).
(4) Cooke, C. J. Bowen, *Some recent developments ...* (1902), p55.

---

(1) *The Times*, 6th June 1906, p5.
(2) Acworth, *The Railways of England*, p59.

18

Another idea which came to nothing was the attempt to employ steam locomotives for canal boat haulage. The Shropshire Union Canal had been leased to the LNWR in 1847 and as most of the system lay in the territory of rival companies (the Cambrian and the Great Western) everything was done to make it prosper.[1] In 1888 the following experiment took place: 'On Wednesday, on the Shropshire Union Canal at Worleston, the LNWR officials tested the experiment of drawing canal boats with a locomotive. A set of rails, 18in gauge and about a mile in length, had been laid along the canal bank. On them was placed a small locomotive of Crewe Works. Two boats were attached by ropes to the locomotive, which drew them along easily at the rate of seven miles an hour. Four boats were then attached, and the same speed was attained. The experiment was deemed successful.'[2]

Despite the confident note of this report there were no further developments on the Shropshire Union Canal but it is interesting to note that locomotive haulage is employed on the Panama Canal (opened 1914).

Much of Webb's inventiveness is associated with the use of cheap steel which was produced at Crewe, the Bessemer process being introduced in 1864 (and abandoned in 1901) and the Siemens-Martin Open Hearth system in the 1870s.[3]

From 1872 steel boilers were produced, which Dr Chaloner says were 'entirely successful'.[4] In 1876 steel frames were used, probably for the first time.[5] Steel fire-boxes were also produced for a period but were found to be unsatisfactory.[6] Webb also introduced 'the making in cast steel of articles which were expensive to forge; and many things also which were formerly made of cast iron are now made of cast steel. The castings embrace such articles as wheels, motion-plates, brackets, horn-blocks, axle-boxes and brake-hangers.'[7]

The LNWR was one of the few railway companies to roll its own rails (another was the Manchester, Sheffield & Lincolnshire Railway).[8]

In the 1880s attempts were made to introduce metal sleepers: 'In 1880 several miles of iron sleepers with wrought-iron chairs riveted on were laid on various portions of the line for experimental purposes, followed, in 1882, by steel sleepers. Between 1880 and 1887, 56 miles had been laid down, of which, however, 44 miles have now been replaced by wooden sleepers, their life having been shorter than anticipated.'[1]

There is a disagreement as to whether the presence of metal sleepers could be detected from the train. Acworth says: 'It is commonly supposed that steel sleepers would make the road less elastic and the vibration and jar of the carriages more perceptible, but the present writer can say, from personal experience, that neither in the carriage nor indeed on the engine of an express train could he perceive any difference, even though he knew he was passing over them.'[2]

An American visitor is more critical: 'I must say I don't like them, they are so noisy. It is plainly discernible when the train drops off the wood on to the steel.'[3]

A more successful development of the permanent way was the introduction of longer rails. Lengths of 30 and 45 feet were usual but about 1896 Webb was responsible for the rolling and adoption of 60 foot length rails. These reduced the number of rail joints and ensured a smoother ride.[4]

Without mentioning either Webb or Crewe, Mr L. T. C. Rolt has praised them by implication in these words: 'The Siemens Martin and Bessemer processes of steel making, employed in conjunction with larger rolling mills, produced steel plates which were both bigger and stronger than the old wrought-iron plates which boiler makers had used hitherto. The new boilers had fewer seams and a greater margin of safety than the iron boilers which they gradually replaced. By the same token, the improvement of permanent way dates from this period, the longer and tougher steel rails taking the place of the old 21-foot iron rails to make possible that smooth high-speed running which we take for granted.'[5]

With all this experience of the manufacture and application of Bessemer steel, Webb became one of its chief advocates. When, in 1875, the Chief Naval Architect of the Royal Navy, Sir Nathaniel Barnaby, criticised it, Webb was able to provide test-pieces and describe how the steel plates were tested.[6] Of the few official letters of Webb that can be traced four are concerned with the provision of specimens of Bessemer steel.[7]

The championing of Bessemer steel is far from the only instance of Webb's respect for the work of other engineers. He was the first locomotive designer to employ David Joy's valve gear (on his 0-6-0 '18 inch'

(1) Photographs survive of two Crewe-built steel canal boats (BR LM Region negatives OS 172 and OS 182). One of them, inevitably, is named *Bessemer*.
(2) *Engineer*, Vol 65 (1888), p436. Note also L. T. C. Rolt, *Inland Waterways of England* (1950), p150, and the unpublished photographic record of the experiment (BR LM Region negatives DM 9016 and DM 10227)
(3) Chaloner, p72.
(4) *ibid*, p72.
(5) Ahrons, *BSRL*, p220
(6) *ibid*, p206.
(7) *Visit of the International Congress of Railway Engineers to Crewe Works ... 1895*, and Ahrons, *BSRL*, p286, who notes that steel castings were introduced in 1880.
(8) Acworth, *The Railways of England*, p62-3, discusses this matter and records the hostility it aroused among the private manufacturers of rails.

(1) *Railway Magazine*, Vol 19 (1906), p184
(2) Acworth, p60.
(3) *Locomotive Engineering*, Dec 1892, p449.
(4) *Railway Magazine*, Vol 54 (1924), p385, gives this information. C. E. R. Sherrington, *A Hundred Years of Inland Transport*, (1934), p216, gives the date of the adoption of the 60 foot length rail as 1894.
(5) L. T. C. Rolt, *Red for Danger*, (1955), p60
(6) Sir Henry Bessemer, *Autobiography* (1905), p249-52.
(7) Two such letters are given in Bessemer's *Autobiography*, p 366-7, and two more are among the collection of Sir William Roberts-Austen, held by the Iron and Steel Institute.

goods engines, built 1880 to 1902), and had a great respect for the work of earlier engineers. He saved at least two pieces of craftsmanship from the scrap-heap: the four cast-iron eagles which still adorn Flag Lane Bridge [1] and one of Richard Trevithick's stationary engines. The latter was shown at the Paris Exhibition of 1889 and was described thus: 'A high-pressure engine designed by R. Trevithick about 1803-9 and made by Hazeldine & Co of Bridgnorth. This engine was found at Hereford in a dismantled state by Mr F. W. Webb of Crewe in 1883, and purchased as scrap iron. The parts were taken to Crewe and put together. Some of the parts were found to be broken; these were mended and a few missing pieces replaced and made to accord as nearly as possible with the illustration in *The Life of Trevithick*.' [2]

Mention must also be made of Webb's restoration and use of such old engines as *Locomotion* and *Cornwall*, both of which were employed on inspection saloons, and his respect for Ramsbottom's 'Lady of the Lake' class. What a contrast to Churchward on the GWR who, in 1906, had both *Lord of the Isles* and *North Star* scrapped.

Mr Dunn endeavoured to find out if Webb received royalties from the LNWR in respect of his patented devices used on their line. Unfortunately, the records of his patent agents, Messrs Haseltine, Lake & Co, were destroyed in the Second World War, but this statement appeared in a summary of Webb's career published at the time of his retirement: 'Although Mr Webb took out many patents, he never received any royalties from the railway company, who, however, in recognition of his services, raised his salary from £5,000, the sum paid to Mr Ramsbottom, to £7,000 a year.' [3]

Surveying Webb's innovations and inventions one is impressed by his originality of thought. For example in the balancing of the driving wheels of his four-cylinder compounds this device was employed: 'In place of the usual crank-shaped centre [of the driving wheels], a large circular boss 2ft 9in in diameter is provided. At the back of this boss a number of recesses are cast, some of which are filled in with lead to form a counter-balance for the high-pressure rods outside ... It will be noticed that the crank webs are extended to form balance weights, so that the whole of the revolving and reciprocating parts are evenly balanced.' [4]

With the originality went the courage to persist with revolutionary ideas. Admittedly this tenacity was disastrous in the case of the Clark and Webb chain brake, [5] but Webb had learned to disregard the critics.

Bessemer steel was supposed to be unreliable and steel boilers were looked upon with distrust until Webb demonstrated otherwise.

He is criticised for persisting with his system of compounding and for not listening to his critics and their suggestions, but systems of compounding were later successful (as the Smith and Smith-Deeley compounds on the Midland Railway) and no one has satisfactorily shown where the Webb system failed.

One is left to wonder why so few of his inventions were adopted and developed, but one obituary writer provides a convincing answer: 'His inventions were legion and covered a very wide field, and though many of them were widely adopted, comparatively few of them have outlived him. But there is nothing extraordinary in that fact. Many of them were most ingenious and most successful and were adopted abroad, though prejudice prevented their adoption on other railways here'. [1]

Webb and the Engineering Institutions.

Webb, as already noticed, was a keen publicist and was always prepared to describe the latest developments on the LNWR to his fellow engineers. He was a life member of the Société des Ingénieurs Civils de France [2], and a member of the Iron and Steel Institute (elected a member in 1874 and a member of Council in 1895), but his main work was for the Institution of Mechanical Engineers and the Institution of Civil Engineers.

He was elected a member of the Institution of Mechanical Engineers in 1862, was a member of Council in 1871 and again in 1875 and was Vice-President in 1877.[3] He was an active member, reading a number of papers and frequently taking part in discussions but in 1885 he resigned and broke off all relations. A possible explanation is that he was disgusted at the heavy criticism of his compounds given in a paper, 'On the consumption of fuel in locomotives' by George Marié, and in the discussion which followed it. Webb was not present and dismissed the criticism in a letter to the Institution: 'he does not propose answering the objections raised to his method of compounding, as he would prefer to let the continued working of the engines show what they are capable of doing.' [4]

H. A. V. Bulleid notes that when the Association of Railway Engineers was founded in 1890 'the only notable abstainer from ... membership was F. W. Webb who refused to join on principle: he would not tolerate a group discussion, but was ready to help individually.' [5] Perhaps his experience with the Mechanical

(1) *Railway Magazine*, Vol 54 (1924), p271, and O. S. Nock, *LNWR*, p58.
(2) *Railroad Gazette*, 1st November 1889.
(3) *Engineer*, Vol 94 (1902), p523. There is also a note in *Railroad Gazette*, Vol 34 (1902), p953: 'We believe that Mr Webb never received any royalties from his company on any of his many patents'.
(4) Charles S. Lake, *The World's Locomotives* (1905), p175; there is also a good photograph of a pair of driving wheels with the balanced crank axle.
(5) O. S. Nock, *LNWR*, p79-84, gives a summary of this unfortunate matter.

(1) *Railway Engineer*, Vol 27 (1906), p201.
(2) Correspondence with the Société has failed to produce any details. 'Nos archives de cette ayant disparu'. (Letter to the author, 28th October 1963)
(3) *The Dictionary of National Biography* entry makes no mention of Webb's membership of the IMechE, which is curious, and I am indebted to the Librarian of the Institution for the details here.
(4) *IMechE*, 1884, p119-21.
(5) H. A. V. Bulleid, *Master Builders of Steam*, p16

Engineers had caused him to assume this attitude.

He had happier relations with the Institution of Civil Engineers. He was made an associate on 23rd May 1865, and became a member on 3rd December 1872. He was elected to council in May 1889 and became a vice-president in November 1900. When he retired from the Council in 1905 he was the senior vice-president.

He gave many papers and often took part in the discussions at the ICE and seemed to be at his ease, even giving such personal details as the following: A boy ought to have served 'as a practical workshop apprentice' before going into the drawing office. 'He was glad that he had been in the position himself.' [1] 'His experience first as a boy, afterwards as a practical riveter, and then as Superintendent of the works ...' [2]

It was to the ICE that Webb told his story of being prepared to line his engines with gold when the Company paid 10 per cent.[3]

Webb does not appear to have objected to criticism from his fellow members of the ICE. His compounds were criticised at a meeting in 1889 when E. Worthington read his paper on 'The compound principle applied to locomotives' [4], a meeting at which Webb was present and in which he contributed to the discussion, but there is no evidence of his being annoyed.

Webb's own writings

IMechE, 1866, p72-4.
Discussion.
Webb on the construction of locomotive boilers.

IMechE, 1866, p280-7.
Paper, by F. W. Webb of Bolton.
Description of a curvilinear shaping machine.
'The object of the writer in designing this machine was to bring the wheels of engines and tenders to a more correct balance ... without ... increasing the cost of production'.
Drawings.

ICE, Vol 37 (1874), p17-20,22,30.
Discussion.
Contribution to discussion of John Robinson's paper in which Webb's arrangement of Giffard injectors was described.

ICE, Vol 41 (1875), p43-5.
Discussion.
Webb on various LNWR topics. Some important views on general design topics, eg he supports use of four driving wheels in place of single-drivers and argues that the latter damage the track.

IMechE, 1875, p 82-3.
Discussion.
Webb on the bearing surfaces between axle-boxes and horn plates on LNWR engines.

(1) *ICE*, Vol 73 (1883), p100.
(2) *ICE*, Vol 81 (1885), p133.
(3) *ICE*, Vol 81 (1885), p135.
(4) *ICE*, Vol 96 (1889), p2-119.

IMechE, 1875, p126-33.
Paper.
Description of a direct-acting circular saw for cutting steel hot. This saw was designed by Ramsbottom but modified by Webb.
Drawings, plates 17-9.

IMechE, 1875, p293-6,303
Discussion.
Webb on the production and uses of steel.

ISI, 1875, p420-1.
Discussion.
Webb on moulds for steel rail ingots.

IMechE, 1877, p182-3,187.
Discussion.
Webb on his enclosed Ramsbottom safety valve.
L. T. C. Rolt has said that 'John Ramsbottom delivered us from evil by inventing a valve which the most ingenious engineman could not alter.' [1] But this entry proves otherwise, for Webb 'had seen the disadvantages of the men being able to tamper with them, as had been done by putting a clip on two or three coils of the spring; and he had endeavoured to get over the difficulty by putting the whole in a closed box, so that no one could get at the spring at all.'

IMechE, 1877, p197-205.
Paper.
On an improved form of slide valve for steam and hydraulic engines.
Drawings, plates 27-30.
Also reported in *Engineer*, Vol 44 (1877), p68-9.

ISI, 1877, p51.
Discussion.
Letter from Webb on the riveting of mild steel.

ISI, 1878, p143-4.
Discussion.
Experiments with Kennedy's spiral punch.

IMechE, 1879, p304-6.
Discussion.
Webb on steel boilers.

IMechE, 1879, p306-13.
Discussion.
Webb on radial axleboxes.

IMechE, 1879, p349-51,353.
Discussion.
Contribution to discussion of Anatole Mallet's paper 'On the compounding of locomotive engines' (p328-47). This is most important as it records Webb's first reaction to compounding. He is cautious: 'He had fitted up an old locomotive ... on the compound system; and he thought he saw elements of success in it, and felt encouraged to try some further experiments'. (p350).

(1) L. T. C. Rolt, *Red for Danger*, p65.

ISI, 1879, p63-4.
Discussion.
Webb on Bessemer steel and its qualities.

IMechE, 1880, p94-5.
Discussion.
Webb on plate rolling.

IMechE, 1880, p432-5,440-1.
(Also letter from Webb reported 1881, p417-8).
Discussion.
Contribution to discussion of David Joy's paper 'On a new reversing and expansive valve-gear'. Webb praises Joy's valve gear and plates 61-3 show Webb's 0-6-0 engine fitted with it.

IMechE, 1881, p260.
Discussion.
Webb on riveted joints.

ISI, 1881, i, p116-17,124
Discussion.
Webb on iron and steel permanent way.

ISI, 1881, i, p141.
Discussion.
Webb on the qualities of Bessemer steel. Steel made by the Bessemer process was as good, he found, as that made by the Siemens-Martin process. Members were free to inspect the Bessemer converter at Crewe 'and if they could find anything wrong, he would be glad if they would tell him about it'.
Note here that the Webb of the 'legend' who 'would tolerate no criticism' is inviting comment.

Engineering, Vol 33 (1882), p156-7.
Paper.
Mr F. W. Webb on railway matters: [report of speech at the annual dinner of the Manchester Association of Employers, Foreman and Draughtsmen].
Outlines the uses of steel by the LNWR and describes the first runs of 'Experiment'.
Also reported in *Engineer*, Vol 53 (1882), p116.

ICE, Vol 73 (1883), p99-101.
Discussion.
Webb describes his method of casting wheels in a revolving mould.

IMechE, 1883, p438-62, (plates 41-4).
Paper.
On compound locomotive engines.
Also reported in:
Engineer, Vol 56 (1883), p92, 97-8, 108.
Engineering, Vol 36 (1883), p125-7.
Railway Engineer, Vol 4 (1883), p189-92.
IMechE, 1884, p119-21.
Discussion.
George Marié's paper 'On the consumption of fuel in locomotives' (p82-101) questioned some details of the Webb compounds, and there was further adverse comment in the discussion that followed. Webb was not present and dismissed the matter in a letter – 'he does not purpose answering the objections raised to his method of compounding, as he would prefer to let the continued working of the engines show what they are capable of doing'. Webb appears to have been offended by this matter as he makes no further contributions to the affairs of the IMechE.

A later paper on compound locomotives by R. Herbert La Page (*IMechE* 1889, p85-147) makes no reference to Webb's compounds, although they are brought into the discussion that follows.

Statistical Society. *Journal*, Vol 47 (1884), p305-6.
Discussion.
Webb on the LNWR.

ICE, Vol 80 (1885), p258-9.
Paper.
Standard engine shed of the LNWR Company. Rugby shed is illustrated, plate 4.

ICE, Vol 1 (1885), p133-6.
Discussion.
Useful account of the development of production methods and Webb's locomotive design policy. The 'official' version of the painting-with-gold story is given on page 135.

ICE, Vol 81 (1885), p299-301.
Paper.
Description of steel permanent way as used on the LNWR.

ICE, Vol 82 (1885), p189-90.
Discussion.
Contribution to discussion of Arthur Moore Thompson's paper 'The signalling of the LNWR' (p166-230) in which Webb's work is outlined.

ISI, 1886, i, p148-50.
Paper.
On the endurance of steel rails.

ICE, Vol 96 (1889), p55-8.
Discussion.
Contribution to discussion of E. Worthington's paper 'The compound principle applied to locomotives' (p2-119) in which Webb's work is discussed. Webb gives a useful outline of his work, and there is an account of the trial of *Compound* on the LSWR (p59-60).
Plates 1-3 contain Webb material.

ISI, 1892, ii, p139-40.
Discussion.
Webb on the use of chrome steel.
ICE, Vol 130 (1897), p178.
Paper.
Permanent way.

This is an abstract of notes only but the paper is also reported in:
Engineer, Vol 83 (1897), p533.
Engineering, Vol 63 (1897), p707,727.

ICE, Vol 133 (1898), p21-4.
Discussion.
Webb on fire-box construction and slide-valves.

ICE, Vol 133 (1898), p302-5.
Paper.
Particulars of various parts of recent LNW locomotives. Descriptions, with drawings, of a fire-box, balanced slide-valve, and other details.

ICE, Vol 138 (1899), p406-11.
Paper.
Compound locomotives.
Also reported in:
Engineer, Vol 87 (1899), p565.
Engineering, Vol 67 (1899), p737, 755.
Railway Engineer, Vol 20 (1899), p212-13.
According to *The Times* this paper 'will always be regarded as a classic contribution to the literature of the subject.' [1]

ICE, Vol 150 (1902), p87-146.
Paper.
Locomotive fire-box stays.

ICE, Vol 149 (1902), p112-15.
Discussion.
Webb on electric traction, towards which he is favourable.

ICE, Vol 147 (1902), p220-1.
Discussion.
Webb on the use of the dynamometer-car and train resistance. He makes reference to managers who demand double-heading under all conditions.

ICE, Vol 155 (1904), p401-10.
Paper.
Copper locomotive-boiler tubes.

Webb's Patents
(in chronological order by date of application).

Improvements in tools or machinery for cutting or shaping metals and other material.
British Patent 287. Application date 3rd February 1864. Accepted 1st August 1864, p6 pl [2].
This is a tool for the 'cutting or forming of curved surfaces when the curves of such surfaces are segments of a circle and when the article operated upon cannot be conveniently moved'.
In this patent the cutting tool is placed in a lever. The plates demonstrate the tool shaping inner rims of locomotive wheels.

(1) *The Times*, 6th June 1906, p5.

Improvements in the manufacture of railway rails.
British Patent 343. Application date 9th February 1864. Accepted 9th August 1864, p4 pl [1].
This patent involves the re-rolling of double-headed rails to produce rails of lighter section.

Improvements in the manufacture of steel tires [sic] for railway wheels.
British Patent 878. Application date 28th March 1865. Accepted 27th September 1863, p5 pl [1].
Casting blank tyres with a 'stalk' (where the axles would be). This 'stalk' is subsequently punched or pressed out.

Improvements in the construction and manufacture of steel crossing for railways, and in the moulds for casting the same, all or parts of which said improvements in moulds are applicable for casting other articles.
British Patent 3332. Application date 23rd December 1865. Accepted 20th June 1866, p7, pl [1].
The steel crossing was formed 'as that the junction of one rail with the point or crossing will overlap its junction with the other rail to about the extent of half the length of a fish plate, so that a fish plate will only be required on one side, as the overlapping rail on the other side will answer the purpose of a fish plate on that side, and by this means also the sudden transition from the rail to the point, or vice versa, is obviated.'
The technique of casting is, first, to cast the point ends deeper than required so that they can then be forged to their required size. This ensures greatest strength at the place of greatest wear. The other technique covered by this patent is to make the moulds in such parts that they can be removed automatically at the required stage of cooling so that the casting can contract freely. The mould is held together with springs and spring levers which are released by bolts and other devices which burn through at the required temperature.

Improvements in machinery and apparatus employed in the manufacture of iron and steel by the Bessemer process.
British Patent 888. Application date 27th March 1867. Accepted 23rd September 1867, p6, pl [1].
This patent, granted to Henry Sharp and to Webb who were both working for the Bolton Iron & Steel Company at this time, covers the general arrangement and position of the converting vessels, improved methods of swivelling them on their axes, improved methods of working the ladle crane, and a locking plate to the gearing for turning the converting vessels.

Improvements in the manufacture of Smiths' anvils.
British Patent 2924. Application date 18th October 1867. Accepted 17th April 1868, p4, pl [1].
Another patent granted to Sharp and Webb. 'Smiths' anvils now in use are generally forged of iron and faced with steel, the horns being welded on; now our invention consists in casting anvils of Bessemer or other cast

steel.' The castings larger than required, are finished by hammering so that all the working surfaces are brought into the condition of forged steel. Alternatively, steel plates can be cast in with the molten steel to provide the harder working surfaces, thus eliminating the forging process.

Improvements in the construction of steam hammers, and in apparatus employed therein.
British Patent 3545. Application date 23rd November 1868. Accepted 20th May 1869, p5, pl [1].
Use of 'Bessemer metal or cast steel' in place of cast or wrought iron then usually employed for them. The patent also covers some simplification of the mechanical parts.

Improvements in locomotive and other steam engines and boilers, parts of which are applicable to riveted work and railway rolling stock in general.
British Patent 3403. Application date 25th November 1869. Accepted 24th May 1870, p9, pl [2].
This long patent covers (a) the making of the inner portion of the fire-box, excepting the top and tube-plate, of a single sheet of iron or steel, (b) making the tube-plate separate from the other part, (c) using oblong rivets, (d) use of Bessemer or cast steel for frames, cross stays and bogie carriages, and consolidating the metal by forging, (e) an improved circular valve, (f) making cases of buffer, draw and bearing springs of cast steel, (g) improved springs consisting of pair of rectangular and other shaped plates, (h) improved springs consisting of conical discs of different diameters combined in sets.

Improvements in mills for rolling and crushing metals and other materials.
British Patent 3747. Application date 27th December 1869. Accepted 25th June 1870, p7, pl.[3]
This patent covers arrangement of the parts of the mill, improved method of applying hydraulic power for setting up the pressing roll so that the power is self contained, a method of applying hydraulic power for raising and lowering the pressing roll and the apparatus for compensating for its traverse motion, and improvements in communicating motion to and reversing the motion of stills.

Improvements in ladles for molten metals.
British Patent 1669. Provisional protection only, 9th June 1870, p2.
Lining metal ladles with 'solid-bricks or blocks of fire-resisting material similar to that used for making crucibles or fire-bricks' instead of the coating of loam then commonly used.

Improvements in locomotive engines and railway breaks [sic].
British Patent 2884. Application date 27th October 1871. Accepted 26th April 1872, p6, pl.[2].
This patent covered (a) the placing of feed pipes within the boiler and connecting them to the injectors or force pumps, (b) using boiler water to apply the brakes, and returning it to the boiler by the pressure of steam used to release the brake-blocks, (c) application of the above braking system to a train of carriages by transmission through a rotating shaft.

Improvements in injectors and arrangements for working the same.
British Patent 2985. Application date 6th November 1871. Accepted 1st May 1872, p6, pl.[1].
Webb's design of injector, 'with an open slot in the body large enough to admit an overflow chamber which embraces the nozzles, and [so arranged] that the same shaft, handle, or lever that opens and closes the overflow cock is also used for adjusting the nozzles.'

Improvements in or applicable to locomotive engines and boilers, parts of which improvements are also applicable to other boilers and to railway carriages.
British Patent 3442. Application date 20th December 1871. Accepted 20th June 1872, p8 pl.[1].
This patent covers (a) construction of axle boxes with the brasses in two halves joined vertically between two side frames, adjustable on screws, (b) the reversing of the cones of the tyres of the centre wheels of engines and carriages having three or more pairs of wheels in a rigid frame, to reduce wear and strain (especially on curves) and to check lateral oscillation on straight track, (c) forming fire-door, air and other holes in fire-boxes by two rings, one of which is forced into the other, (d) design of glass tube water 'gauge'.

Improvements in locomotive engines.
British Patent 3748. Provisional protection only, 19th November 1873, p2.
Condensing system for engines working in tunnels or under-ground railways, automatically brought into operation from the track.

Improvements in mechanism or arrangements for actuating railway points and signals.
British Patent 442. Application date 4th February 1874. Accepted 3rd August 1874, p7, pl.[1].
'An improved combination, arrangement, and construction of mechanism for holding the point and signal levers, and locking the same in their correct positions.'

Improvements in mechanism or arrangements for actuating railway points and signals.
British Patent 494. Application date 7th February 1874. Accepted 4th August 1874, p9, pl.[2].
A complete system as in 442.

Improvements in injectors.
British Patent 1135. Application date 1st April 1874. Accepted 26th September 1874, p4, pl.[1].
'Instead of making ... discharging and receiving "cones" or "nozzles" in two distinct parts, with a space or break between them to form an overflow, the two nozzles or cones are made continuous, and without break or overflow orifice or chamber.'

Improvements in mechanism or arrangements for actuating and interlocking railway points and signals.
British Patent 3916. Application date 13th November 1874. Accepted 8th May 1875, p10, pl [2].
Yet another complete system. It includes the combination of weight levers with an oscillating frame connected with a signal, so that any required number of signalmen may have control over the same signal.

Improvements in mechanism or arrangements for actuating railway points and signals.
British Patent 462. Application date 6th February 1875. Accepted 27th July 1875, p9, pl [2].
Improvements to the system covered by British Patent 442 of 4th February 1874.

Improvements in mechanism for actuating and locking railway points and signals.
British Patent 206. Application date 19th January 1876. Accepted 7th July 1876, p4, pl [2].
'Hitherto railway points have been locked by belts entering holes or slots in a cross bar connecting the two point rails, and in case of breakage of the connections the pointsman might suppose that the points were correctly locked when in fact the broken connection only was locked. The object of my Invention is to simultaneously and separately lock both rails of a pair of points when in their correct position the signals, by connection with the point mechanism, being locked and unlocked by the lever handle locking mechanism in the order required, the point mechanism and signals being also at the same time locked while a train is passing the points.'

Improvements in mechanism or arrangements for interlocking railway points and signals.
British Patent 2352. Application date 6th June 1876. Accepted 28th November 1876, p5, pl [2].
An improved system for locking the levers of railway points and signals.

Improvements in apparatus for applying the brakes and giving notice to the drivers, firemen and guards on approaching or passing signals at danger or caution, and in arrangements for automatically showing by the lights the direction in which an engine is travelling.
British Patent 167. Application date 12th January 1877. Accepted 5th July 1877, p6, pl [2].
This patent outlines (a) a system of actuating self-acting continuous brakes when a train is passing a signal 'at danger' or 'caution', (b) a method of actuating self-acting brakes, whistles or gongs, singly or simultaneously, when passing signals at 'danger' or 'caution' by the use of elastic props, (c) a system of actuating lamps or shades before lamps on locomotives by connection with the reversing lever or its mechanism to show a 'colour' corresponding to the direction in which the engine is to move.
This would appear to be an early and untried (?) form of Automatic Train Control system. [1]

Improvements in brake apparatus for railway vehicles.
British Patent 691. Application date 20th February 1878. Accepted 19th August 1878, p7, pl [4].
'System ... of actuating brakes by differential pistons and cylinders, or differential bellows, or like apparatus, where the pressure or partial vacuum acts in one direction simultaneously on both pistons or bellows and when this pressure or vacuum ceases to act, the pistons or bellows re-act in consequence of the pressure or vacuum reserved in one of the cylinders or bellows.'

Improvements in boilers and wheels for locomotives and other vehicles, parts of which improvements are applicable to other purposes.
British Patent 692. Application date 20th February 1878. Accepted 19th August 1878, p5, pl [1].
This patent covers (a) a method of constructing the hole for fire-box doors, (b) a design of fire-box stay, where the stays are tubular and fix in taper holes, (c) design of fusible plug in which there is a yet smaller and more fusible plug to give earlier warning, (d) method of making joints of cylinder covers, valve chests, pipes, covers, lids, and where joints have to be made between two surfaces by the combination of a compressed tubular ring retained in a dove-tail groove, (e) method of securing 'tyres' on the rims of railway wheels.

Improvements in brake apparatus for railway vehicles, and in signalling on railway trains from passengers to guards or drivers, or between guard and driver.
British Patent 693. Application date 20th February 1878. Accepted 19th August 1878, p8, pl [3].
Modifications to British Patent 691 of 20th February 1878 to enable carriages to be used on trains with different braking systems. The brakes are actuated by chains, wire or ropes along the length of train, and friction drums. Also covered by the patent is a system of giving signals on trains by reducing the pressure or vacuum in pipes for actuating brakes, passing along a train to a fixed extent.

Improvements in slide valves and valve ports or facings for steam and other motive engines.
British Patent 3289. Application date 21st August 1878. Accepted 20th February 1879, p6, pl [1].
This patent covers (a) a circular valve free to rotate in its buckle, combined with port faces formed with extended clearance spaces and lubrication spaces, thus the valve rotates and wear is even instead of causing grooves, (b) combination of an equilibrium valve, through the interior of which steam is admitted to the cylinder, with the improved circular or ordinary slide valves for compound engines, (c) arrangement of rectangular slide valves so as to be moved laterally when the pressure of steam fluctuates and so avoid grooving.

(1) The GWR first tried ATC on the Henley branch in 1906. See Simmons, *Railways of Britain*, p169.

Improvements in staff apparatus for controlling the traffic on single line railways.
British Patent 962. Application date 18th January 1892. Accepted 28th May 1892, p5, pl [4 in 2].
Modification to the system covered by British Patent 1263 of 23rd January 1889, enabling the temporary closing of certain stations or block posts.
This is a joint patent with Arthur Moore Thompson.

Improvements in apparatus for controlling the traffic on single-line railways.
British Patent 13,122. Application date 18th July 1892. Accepted 8th April 1893, p3, pl [2 in 1].
Modification to the system covered by British Patent 12199 of 3rd August 1890, which substitutes 'a receptacle for tickets in connection with the staff or tablet apparatus itself, instead of having the tickets in connection with the staff or tablet itself.'
A joint patent with Arthur Moore Thompson.

Improvements in apparatus for closing an electric circuit by the passage of a locomotive or train over a line of railway, and recording apparatus connected therewith.
British Patent 20,488. Application date 12th November 1892. Accepted 21st October 1893, p3, pl [1].
This device, patented with Arthur Moore Thompson, works by the depression of the rail. It can be employed to record the passing of the train at the signal cabin.

Improved method of forming junctions between electric light cables and electric lamps.
British Patent 21,243. Application date 22nd November 1892. Accepted 2nd September 1893, p2, pl [1].
This patent, submitted with Arthur Moore Thompson, covers the formation of junctions between electric light cables and electric lamps by means of a metal screw forced into contact with the copper core of the cable, combined with a porcelain box or cover-piece containing the necessary fuse wires and lamp terminals.

Self-acting anti-vacuum valves for locomotive cylinders.
British Patent 4180. Application date 25th February 1893. Accepted 23rd December 1893, p2, pl [1].
This device enables air to be freely drawn into the cylinders preferably through the steam chest or chests, when the engine is running with the steam shut off, and thus free the movement of the pistons which is now more or less retarded by their effort to create a vacuum.

Expansion etc gear for locomotives.
This application, 4344 of 28th February 1893, was abandoned and so was not printed.

Improvement in locomotive, marine and other boilers.
British Patent 7556. Application date 13th April 1893. Accepted 17th March, 1894, p2, pl [1].
This patent covers a smokebox tube-plate made in two parts, an outer and inner one, the outer being firmly secured to the boiler and having a packing device for making a joint, the inner, which carries the ends of the tubes, being loose and free to slide in the outer part.

Railway carriage lavatories.
This application, 12087 of 20th June 1893, was abandoned and so was not printed.

Improvements in locomotive and other steam boilers.
British Patent 13,547. Application date 13th July, 1894. Accepted 11th May 1895, p2, pl [1].
This patent covers:
(i) the drilling of small holes into, but not through, the water side of the tube plate 'to equalise the section of the metal between the tubes and at the same time keep the tube plate cooler.'
(ii) A method of fixing tubes so that the ends on the outside of the plate are not burned away by the fire. This is done by recessing the tube plate to take the beading on the tubes.

Locomotives.
This application, 14432 of 27th July 1894, was abandoned and so was not printed.

Improvements in water gauge attachments for steam boilers.
British Patent 6208. Application date 26th March, 1895. Accepted 18th January 1896, p3, pl [2 in 1].
Two means of preventing the scattering of glass when water gauges burst, the first by encasing the glass in spiral wire-spring, and the other by encasing it in a guard or shield of thin sheet metal.

Steam brake and coupling gear for locomotives.
This application, 13748 of 17th July 1895, was abandoned and so was not printed.

Propelling bicycle or tricycle.
This application, 3259 submitted 'with another' on 13th February 1896, was abandoned and so was not printed.

Improvements in or connected with railway rail joints.
British Patent 25,496. Application date 13th November 1896. Accepted 7th August 1897, p2, pl [2 in 1].
This patent covers combined joint chair and splice in halves, wherein three bolts of large size are employed for securing the parts without weakening the rail by drilling large holes through the web.

Improvements in the valve gear of locomotive engines.
British Patent 29,239. Application date 21st December 1896. Accepted 6th November 1897, p2, pl [1].
Method of working the valves of two cylinders of a four-cylinder locomotive engine with one set of eccentrics and links or other suitable expansion and reversing gear.[1]

(1) E. C. Poultney, *British Express Locomotive Development*, (1952) p37.

Improvements in the construction and working of loco-motive engines and boilers.
British Patent 29,240. Application date 21st December 1896. Accepted 6th November 1897, p3, pl [2].
'The dividing of the smoke box of a locomotive boiler into two independent compartments, each compartment enclosing a portion of the discharge ends of the tubes and providing each compartment with a separate blast pipe and chimney.' [1]

Improvements in steam generators.
British Patent 29,638. Application date 24th December 1896. Accepted 11th September 1897, p4, pl [1].
A design of flash boiler, jointly patented with Arthur Moore Thompson.

Piston valves.
This application, 3993 of 15th February 1897, was abandoned and so was not printed.

Handle bar.
This application, 9610 of 15th April 1897, was abandoned and so was not printed.

Improvements in apparatus for working railway points and signals by electric power.
British Patent 12,128. Application date 17th May 1897. Accepted 2nd April 1898, p7, pl [6 in 4].
This patent, granted to Webb and Arthur Moore Thompson, used a miniature form of the ordinary interlocking frame.

Improvements in and connected with apparatus for controlling the traffic on single lines of railway.
British Patent 18,259. Application date 5th August 1897. Accepted 18th December 1897, p7, pl [1].
This patent, granted to Webb and A. M. Thompson and George Edwards of the Railway Signal Co Ltd, Fazakerley, Liverpool, developed apparatus covered by British Patent 1263 (of 23rd January 1889) and British Patent 9084 (of 12th June 1890). It covered making the electric connection or line by which the instruments are electrically operated capable of use also for transmitting telephonic messages, substituting a magneto-electric generator for the batteries hitherto used for generating the electric current and the provision of staffs such that several trains can be despatched successively from one end of a section to the other end when required whilst still not allowing of a further staff being removed until all the trains so despatched have passed over the section. Finally provision was made for sending an engine along a portion of a section, to render banking assistance, for example.

Improvements in the arrangement of buffers for railway vehicles.
British Patent 5982. Application date 11th March 1898. Accepted 21st January 1899, p2, pl [1].
This was an arrangement of rolling stock buffers 'to prevent undue pressure on the inner buffers of coupled vehicles when passing round curves.'

Improvements in apparatus for working railway points and signals by electricity.
British Patent 6052. Application date 20th March 1899. Accepted 27th January 1900, p5, pl [3 in 2].
Granted to Webb and A. M. Thompson, this patent contained modifications to British Patent 12128 (of 17th May 1897) 'to provide an improved apparatus for actuating points more especially points to sidings over which shunting is performed and requiring quick movement and the avoidance of damage to the points and the actuating apparatus should the points be run through.'

Railway points and signals.
This application, 20903 of 19th October 1899, submitted by Webb 'with another', was abandoned and so was not printed.

Railway points and signals.
This application, 4320, submitted by Webb 'with another' on 7th March 1900, was abandoned and so was not printed.

Improvements in the form of bricks used for building purposes.
British Patent 12,357. Application date 18th June 1901. Accepted 28th September 1901, p [1], [2 in 1].
Bricks, with upper and lower faces at an angle to prevent the passage of rain or moisture in the joints.

Improvements in apparatus for working railway points and signals by electric power.
British Patent 27,090. Application date 9th December 1902. Accepted 18th June 1903, p4, pl [3 in 2].
Modifications and additions to British Patent 12,128 (of 17th May 1897), granted to Webb and A. M. Thompson.

Webb's Inventions
(abandoned patents are not included as details are not available).
General
Ahrons, E. L.
The British Steam Railway Locomotive, 1825-1925
Locomotive Publishing Co, 1927 (photo reprint 1960).
A valuable source for details of many of the inventions. Drawings are often provided.

SLS, Vol 34 (1958), p201-5.
Clifford, G. H. W.,
'Some notes on F. W. Webb's engines.'
An important article which stresses Webb's metallurgical and other pioneering work. It also provides a good summary of the Webb innovations on engines.

(1) E. C. Poultney, *British Express Locomotive Development*, (1952) p38.

Anti-vacuum valves
British Patent 4180: 25th February 1893.

Automatic train control
British Patent 167: 12th January 1877.

Axle-boxes and the double radial truck [1]
British Patent 3442: 20th December 1872.
British Patent 5052: 24th October 1882.
Engineering, Vol 14 (1872), p421.
'Axle-box for locomotive engines, designed by Mr F. W. Webb'
Railway Engineer, Vol 23 (1902), p101-2.
'Webb's double radial truck and radial axle-box'

Boile-tube cutting tool
British Patent 19479: 4th December 1889.

Boilers
British Patent 3403: 25th November 1869.
British Patent 1974: 9th February 1888.
British Patent 3712: 2nd March 1891.
British Patent 7556: 13th April 1893.
British Patent 13547: 13th April 1894.
British Patent 29638: 24th December 1896.
Engineering, Vol 13 (1872), p423-4.
'Locomotive boiler mountings and feeding apparatus, designed by Mr F. W. Webb'
Engineering, Vol 15 (1873, p334-5.
Steel locomotive boiler at the International Exhibition: [Vienna, 1873].
Engineering, Vol 28 (1879), p264, (illus 257).
Steel locomotive boiler.
Engineer, Vol 68 (1889), p326, 479, (illus p328, 478).
Webb's steel boilers: [8-type].

Brakes [2]
British Patent 2884: 27th October 1871.
British Patent 691: 20th February 1878.
British Patent 693: 20th February 1878.
British Patent 1892: 13th May 1879.
British Patent 16447: 15th December 1886.
British Patent 1686: 4th February 1888.
Engineering, Vol 25 (1878), p46, 104.
'Clark and Webb's brake'
Engineer, Vol 63 (1887), p335-6.
Mr F. W. Webb on railway brakes: [leader].
Strong words to Mr Webb.
LRCWR, Vol 45 (1939), p278-80.
Branston, C. A. 'F. W. Webb and the brake question'
An important article.
Railway Press, (10.5.1890).
[Discussion in the brake controversy].
Railway Magazine, Vol 81 (1937), p143-4.
[Brake arrangements on] Webb locomotives of the LNWR.

(1) See also Ahrons' criticism of the Webb radial axles, *LTWNC*, p36.
(2) See also Ahrons, *LTWNC*, p34-5.

Buffers
British Patent 5982: 11th March 1898.
Engineering News, (24th January 1891).
'The Webb system of hydraulic buffers'
Engineer, Vol 86 (1898), p91.
'Webb's equalising buffer arrangement for railway vehicles'
Engineering, Vol 66 (1898), p66, 472.
'Buffer equalising arrangement'
Railway Engineer, Vol 19 (1898), p161-2.
'F. W. Webb's equalising buffer arrangement'

Building bricks
British Patent 12357: 18th June 1901.

Carriage door opener
British Patent 11321: 23rd September 1885.
British Patent 14632: 11th November 1886.
Railway Magazine, Vol 20 (1907), p393-4.
'Webb's patent railway carriage door opener'

Carriage frame
Engineering, Vol 39 (1885), p670-2.
Frame for 42ft saloon carriage.

Carriage heating
British Patent 3152: 20th July 1881.

Combustion chamber
British Patent 3712: 2nd March 1891.

Compound locomotives
Inventions associated with.
British Patent 1128: 16th March 1881.
British Patent 4738: 12th March 1884.
British Patent 16608: 15th November 1888.
British Patent 701: 14th January 1889.

Crank shaft.
Engineer, Vol 81 (1896), p451.
A built-up locomotive crankshaft [letter from Webb]:
'The crank ... was for one of our engines with 17 inch cylinders by 24 inch stroke.'
Engineering, Vol 61 (1896), p590.
Built-up locomotive crank axle.

Double chimney
British Patent 29240: 21st December 1896.
Locomotive Magazine, Vol 2 (1897), p106
Double chimney engine, LNWR. [*Hampden*].
LRCWR, Vol 48 (1942), p215-6.
'The Coming of the extended smokebox'
Useful article, well illustrated.

Electric wiring junctions
British Patent 21243: 22nd November 1892.

Engine shed
Engineering, Vol 33 (1882), p240-1.
Standard engine shed.

Engineering, Vol 63 (1897), p277, (illus p276).
'Through and through' engine shed at Crewe. There is also a note on Webb's method of construction on p311. Ironwork and woodwork were made strictly to template, thus reducing the cost of erection.

Fireboxes
British Patent 3403: 25th November 1869.
British Patent 3442: 20th December, 1872
British Patent 692: 20th February 1878.
British Patent 1974: 9th February 1888.
Engineering, Vol 10 (1870), p436.
Method of constructing locomotive fireboxes, designed by Mr F. W. Webb, Engineer, Bolton.
Engineering, Vol 15 (1873), p49.
Fireholes of locomotive boilers [designed by Webb].
Engineering, Vol 47 (1889), p559, (illus p 562).
Webb's locomotive firebox.
Engineering, Vol 48 (1889), p234.
'Corrugated steel locomotive firebox'

Friction gear
Locomotive Magazine, Vol 9 (1903), p350.
Combined brake and coupling gear.

Injectors
British Patent 2985: 6th November 1871.
British Patent 1135: 1st April 1874.
Engineering, Vol 14 (1872), p188.
Injectors for locomotive engines, designed by Mr F. W. Webb.
Engineering, Vol 39 (1885), p467, (illus p479).
Webb's injector and clack box for locomotives.

Permanent way
British Patent 343: 9th February 1864.
British Patent 3332: 23rd December 1865.
British Patent 3549: 4th September 1879.
British Patent 35496: 13th November 1896.
Engineering, Vol 31 (1881), p5, (illus p7).
'Webb's steel and iron permanent way'
Engineering, Vol 39 (1885), p497, (illus 491).
Webb's steel permanent way.
Engineering, Vol 64 (1897), p303.
'Railway chair for the LNWR'
Railroad Gazette, Vol 19 (1887), p450-2.
'Permanent way: LNWR'

Piston Valves
British Patent 1378: 26th January 1891.

Rolling Mills
British Patent 3747: 27th December 1869.
Engineering, Vol 11 (1871), p185.
'Rolling mill for tyres and hoops, etc, designed by Mr F. W. Webb, Engineer, Bolton.
Engineer, Vol 42 (1876), p13-4, (illus p10).
'Siemens' Steel Works, Landore: tyre rolling mill, designed by Mr F. W. Webb'
Engineering, Vol 22 (1876), p358-60.

'The rail mill at Crewe [designed by Webb]'

Safety valve
Engineering, Vol 13 (1881), p454.
'Standard safety valve'
Modified Ramsbottom valve used on all Webb engines.

Screw reverse gear
British Patent 4738: 12th March 1884.
British Patent 701: 14th January 1889.

Shaping tool
British Patent 287: 3rd February 1864.

Signalling apparatus
British Patent 442: 4th February 1874.
British Patent 494: 7th February 1874.
British Patent 3916: 13th November 1874.
British Patent 462: 6th February 1875.
British Patent 206: 19th January 1876.
British Patent 2352: 6th June 1876.
British Patent 12128: 17th May 1897.
British Patent 6052: 20th March 1899.
British Patent 27090: 9th December 1902.
Railway Engineer, Vol 3 (1882), p148-9.
[Webb's interlocking apparatus].
Engineering, Vol 40 (1885), p468, (illus p 472).
The LNWR signals.
Railroad Gazette, Vol 33 (1901), p24-5.
'The Webb and Thompson electric switch and signal apparatus'
Railway Engineer, Vol 22 (1901), p40-3, 68.
'The Webb and Thompson electric point and signal apparatus'
Railway Magazine, Vol 10 (1902), p67-74.
'SEMAPHORE'.
Signalling and interlocking: its growth and development, part 2.
Includes a description of the Webb and Thompson system.

Slide valves
British Patent 3403: 25th November 1869.
British Patent 3289: 21st August 1878.
Engineering, Vol 10 (1870), p372.
Equilibrium slide valve, designed by Mr F. W. Webb, Engineer, Bolton.
Engineering, Vol 10 (1870), p372.
Webb's circular slide valve as fitted to Messrs Aveling and Porter's traction engine.

Smiths' anvils
British Patent 2924: 18th October 1867.
Springs
British Patent 3403: 25th November 1869.

Staff and tablet apparatus
British Patent 1263: 23rd January 1889.
British Patent 12199: 5th August 1890.

British Patent 962: 18th January 1892.
British Patent 13122: 18th July 1892.
British Patent 18259: 5th August 1897.
Engineering, Vol 49 (1890), p562-3.
Webb and Thompson's staff apparatus.
Railroad Gazette, Vol 22 (1890), p536-7, 542.
Webb and Thompson's train staff apparatus.
Railroad Gazette, Vol 28 (1896), p702-3.
The Webb and Thompson train-staff apparatus.

Steam condensing system for locomotives
British Patent 3745: 19th November 1873.

Steam hammers
British Patent 3545: 23rd November 1868.

Steel making
British Patent 888: 27th March 1867.
British Patent 1669: 9th June 1870.

Valve gear
British Patent 29239: 21st December 1896.
Water gauges
British Patent 3442: 20th December 1872.
British Patent 6208: 26th March 1895.
Engineering, Vol 15 (1873), p36.
'Gauge-glass fittings designed by Mr F. W. Webb'
Engineer, Vol 81 (1896), p34.

Glass water gauge protector: [letter from Webb].
Engineering, Vol 61 (1896), p98.
Railway Engineer, Vol 18 (1896), p40.
'Webb's patent water-gauge glass guard'

Wheels
British Patent 287: 3rd February 1864.
British Patent 878: 28th March 1865.
British Patent 3442: 20th December 1872.
British Patent 692: 20th February 1878.
Engineering, Vol 17 (1874), p30.
Webb's curvilinear slotting machine [for wheel finishing].
Engineering, Vol 31(1881), p590.
'Cast-iron wheels'

Further details of Webb's inventions are to found in the list of his IMechE and ICE papers on pages 21-23.

2c - The Locomotives

*'I am not so much concerned in excessively high rates
of speed as in getting a very heavy train along the
line with one engine at a reasonable speed'.*

F. W. Webb, *Railway Magazine*, Vol 6 (1900), p102.

Webb's locomotives have been adequately discussed in a number of books and periodical articles. It will merely be necessary here to give an outline appraisal and to pay some attention to those facets of the subject that have been neglected.

The LNWR offered wide scope to the locomotive designer. He had to maintain a force of some 2,620 engines [1] to work the 2,700 miles over which the Company had running powers [2] at a rate of some 39,142,315 train miles each year.[3] He was required to provide fast engines to work the 'Scotch Expresses' and the 'Irish Mail' at competitive speeds, powerful engines to handle the Welsh coal traffic, and engines for branch line work and such specialised duties as shunting and dock work.

Webb inherited a small engine policy which had been established from the earliest days of the London & Birmingham Railway by Edward Bury and continued at Crewe in the time of Alexander Allan (J. E. McConnell's large engine policy at Wolverton being dismissed when locomotive construction ceased there). This policy never became an embarrassment to John Ramsbottom but during Webb's time the weight of trains increased rapidly, for example, 'between 1872 and 1889 the tare weight of the standard LNW carriage had increased by 80 per cent, namely from 10 to 18 tons.' [4] Webb tried to meet the new demands and pioneered the larger boiler[5] and higher boiler pressures[6], but he was unable to design an engine adequate for the task. Sherrington has noted: 'There were periods when the locomotive power on some of the railways became temporarily overwhelmed by the train-loading, notably on the LNW at the time of Mr Webb's retirement in 1903.' [7] In October 1901 the General Manager, Frederick Harrison, imposed the 'equals 17' rule upon Webb, which directed that every train of more than 270 tare tons weight had to be double-headed, regardless of booked times, gradients or class of engine.

Despite these circumstances many of Webb's most economically successful engines were small. The 'Jumbos', the '17in Coal Engine' and the '18in Goods' were all compact little locomotives, cheap to build and dependable to run. The performances of *Hardwicke* (which in the Race to the North in August 1895 ran more than 140 miles at an average speed of nearly 70 mph) and *Charles Dickens* (which completed one million miles in 9 years 216 days, and two million miles in 20 years 73 days) show that the small size did not prevent record performances.

Long after Webb's compounds had disappeared some of the Webb simple engines were still in use. Norman Marlow has described the working of 'Jumbos' (including *Hardwicke*) in the thirties [1], and the working of a 2-4-2 tank in 1947.[2] The first '18in Goods' engine (originally No. 2365, later LMS No. 8333, and finally BR No. 58363) was still in service in 1950 [3] and O. S. Nock has described a run on another member of that class (No. 38, later BR No. 58396) during that same year.[4] There were fourteen Webb engines still at work in 1955 [5], but by the 1958 edition of the *Observer's Book of Railway Locomotives of Britain* only four were still in service: the 0-6-2 Coal Tank No. 58926, which has been preserved, and the three 0-6-0 'Special Tank' engines (Nos. 3, 6 and 7) which were employed shunting at Wolverton carriage works.

We must now turn our attention to Webb's attempts to adapt the principle of compounding to the locomotive. Despite J. H. Clapham's suggestion that this was inspired by American practice [6], Webb actually followed the example of French engineers. Anatole Mallet had introduced three compound locomotives of the two-cylinder type on the Bayonne & Biarritz Railway in July 1879. Webb attended Mallet's lecture on compounding which was read to the Institution of Mechanical Engineers in 1879 [7] and was able to report that 'he had fitted up an old locomotive ... on the compound system; and he thought that he saw elements of success in it, and felt encouraged to try some further experiments.' [8]

(1) *Locomotive Engineering*, (Dec 1892), p449.
(2) *ibid.*
(3) George Findlay, *Working and Management of an English Railway* (2nd ed, 1889), p151. The figure quoted refers to the year 1888.
(4) C. E. R. Sherrington, *A Hundred Years of Inland Transport*, p222.
(5) G. Montague, *Ten Years of Locomotive Progress*, p51-5: 'These [the 0-8-0s] were the first engines ... to be fitted with the modern long boiler'. (p147)
(6) E. C. Poultney *British Express Locomotive Development*, p 114. 'There seems no doubt that the higher pressures used by Webb for his compounds, attracted attention to the use of increased steam pressures'.
(7) C. E. R. Sherrington, *ibid*, p279.

(1) Norman Marlow, *Footplate and Signal Cabin* (1956), p56-7.
(2) *ibid*, p 58-9.
(3) O. S. Nock, *Premier Line*, p75.
(4) *ibid*, p77-8. See also O. S. Nock's *Four Thousand Miles on the Footplate*, (1952) p160-2 for another account.
(5) *Railway Magazine*, Vol 101 (1955), p680.
(6) J. H. Clapham, *An Economic History of Modern Britain* (1938), Vol 3, p349. Clapham also makes the mistake of supposing this to be 'the only system of compounding which was ever much adopted in England'.
(7) *IMechE*, 1879, p349-51, 353.
(8) *ibid*, p350.

The old locomotive was an Allan Crewe-type 2-2-2 engine which Webb had adapted to the Mallet two-cylinder principle in 1879. It worked on the Nuneaton and Ashby branch for a time and the economy of coal obviously impressed Webb. He did not pursue the two-cylinder method, however, but developed the three-cylinder system (with two high-pressure cylinders and one low-pressure cylinder) which had been conceived but not developed by Jules Morandière in 1866.[1] It was this system that Webb was to employ until he experimented with the four-cylinder compound engine.

Before dismissing the Allan single which Webb used for his early experiments (by this time numbered 1874, but originally No. 54 *Medusa*) it must be recorded that in 1895 it was converted into a triple expansion engine, probably the only triple expansion locomotive ever built, and renamed *Triplex*. It was the stand-by engine for Mr Webb's private coupé but Webb's driver, Harry Castlebar, did not like it.[2] It was broken up in 1903.

The first of the three-cylinder compounds, *Experiment*, appeared in 1882 [3] and the reaction of *The Engineer* will show the decline in the fortune of Webb's system of compounding. In its number for 10th February 1882 *Experiment* is greeted with a verbal fanfare and enthusiastic support for Webb's project. The first small doubts appear in a leader of 14th September 1883, and in the leader of 15th February 1884, all support is withdrawn: 'The compound locomotive does not appear to grow in favour with locomotive superintendents ... The results up to the present are not encouraging'. This leader examines all the evidence and finds the compounds wanting: 'Mr Webb has carried out a most interesting and instructive experiment.' [4]

This polite dismissal of the compounds contrasts with the bitter attacks in the correspondence columns of the engineering journals. 'Anti-Compound' made his attacks in *The Engineer*, writing on 2nd April 1886, 'It is, I think, quite clear now that the Webb engines are complete failures', while 'Argus' made his monumental attack in the pages of *Engineering*.

The 'Argus' letters are worthy of some attention if only because of the acrimony, tenacity and industry with which the writer attacked the Webb compounds. Mr Dunn has estimated that, on the basis of 855 words to an average *Engineering* column, 'Argus' expended 32,573 words in eleven letters:

Issue	Col	Words	Issue	Col	Words
11.9.1885	4	3420	20.11.1885	4	3420
25.9.1885	2¼	1923	9.12.1885	2½	2122
9.10.1885	4	3420	18.12.1885	4	3420
23.10.1885	4	3420	1.1.1886	4	3420
30.10.1885	2¼	1923	1.1.1886	4	3420
13.11.1885	3	2565			

(1) *ICE*, Vol 96 (1889), p12.
(2) *Railway Magazine*, Vol 54 (1924), p274-5: other information on *Triplex* will be found in Ahrons, *BSRL*, p293-4.
(3) Steel, p462, gives an account of the trial run of *Experiment* and shows Webb's almost childish impatience to get his new engine into service.
(4) *Engineer*, Vol 53 (1882), p104-5; Vol 56 (1883), p210; Vol 57 (1884), p132.

Mr Dunn also tried to identify 'Argus'. He corresponded with the present editor of *Engineering* who was able to tell him that Webb's opponent 'was the representative, in India, of the Baldwin-Lima-Hamilton Corporation, USA (or, as I believe the organization was known at the time, of Burnham, Parry, Williams & Co). As far as I know, he was an Englishman, or at least a Briton'. In a later letter he told Mr Dunn that 'the identity of "Argus" was known to F. W. Webb'. Unfortunately, his identity was not known to the present editor.

Webb took no part in this correspondence, his only comment being to name one of his 'Dreadnought' three-cylinder compounds (No. 2056) *Argus*. The controversy over the compounds continued. As would be expected, Webb's associates were enthusiastic defenders of the compounds [1] but independent judges have tended to be critical. Acworth did not like them [2] and an American visitor dismissed them politely with the words: 'Of the compounds I am loath to speak ... Whatever may be said, their inventor does not hesitate to put them on heavy fast trains.' [3] Ahrons, that staunch GWR man, had little praise for them but admitted that he was 'genuinely sorry' when the 'Teutonics' were scrapped.[4]

No critic of the compounds was as severe and thorough as Webb's successor, George Whale, who, in a short reign of six years (1903-1909), scrapped or converted the majority of them. By the time Webb died (1906), all the 'Experiments' and 'Dreadnoughts' had gone, and some of the 'Teutonics'. Some of the compounds survived the massacre by being simplified: the 'Alfred the Great' class reappeared as 'Benbows', the 'Jubilees' became 'Renowns' and the three-cylinder 0-8-0s emerged as two-cylinder simples. Webb's four-cylinder 0-8-0 coal engines, the best of his compounds, were among the few survivors, some indeed being built in Whale's time. Sixty of them were still compounded in 1923.[5] Ironically, the last three-cylinder compound was the least worthy of survival. It was 'John Hick' class No. 1505 *Richard Arkwright*, which was not scrapped until 1912.[6] Dr Tuplin comments: 'The 'John Hicks' have always been so bad that there was very little work to which anyone dare apply them. Thus they never had anything arduous to do and this may explain why one of them lasted till 1912.' [7]

The controversy continues, flaring up occasionally in the railway magazines, for example, in the *Locomotive, Railway Carriage and Wagon Review* in 1950. After many years of investigation and argument, however,

(1) C. J. Bowen Cooke, *British Locomotives* (1893), p299, and the same author's *Some Recent Developments ...*, p40: George Findlay, *Working and Management of an English Railway*, p 103.
(2) W. M. Acworth, *The Railways of England*, p69-70.
(3) *Locomotive Engineering*, (Dec 1892), p453.
(4) Ahrons, *LTWNC*, p37.
(5) O. S. Nock, *Premier Line* p123.
(6) *ibid*, p102.
(7) W. A. Tuplin, *North Western Steam* (1963), p48.

the questions still remain unanswered; were the compounds indeed failures, despite the performances of the 'Teutonic' class engines *Ionic* and *Adriatic* for example? If they were failures, what was the reason? Were the drivers responsible, in part, for failing to adapt themselves to a new type of engine? [1] A solution to these problems will be difficult to find, for the evidence of the past is prejudiced and there is little modern engineering research likely to provide any additional information on the Webb system of compounding.

Although Whale brought about the end of compounding on the LNWR, it was successfully employed on other railways, notably in this country, on the Midland Railway. Even Sir Nigel Gresley had one engine (the remarkable No. 10000) running as a four-cylinder compound at one time. It was superheating and the GWR-type taper boiler, however, that were to bring about the great developments in the use of steam that the advocates of compounding had hoped to introduce.

Little attempt has been made to assess Webb's part in the general design and appearance of LNWR locomotives. His contribution was of two kinds: he retained some basic 'Family' characteristics – the rectangular rear wheel splasher on the passenger engines, for example – and he added some features which were to become LNWR 'trade-marks'. The chimney which Webb introduced in 1872 demonstrates this: the square base is inherited from Ramsbottom but Webb has added the distinctive iron cap, a simplification of the older engineer's decoration. The Webb chimney 'appeared in one form or another on every subsequent locomotive until 1922.' [2]

Dr Tuplin has stated that Webb initiated 'a neat external style that lasted as long as the North Western Railway' [3], and this can be seen when we compare the two photographs of the engine *John Ramsbottom* (No. 1211) where one photograph shows the engine as originally built and the other as it was re-built by Webb.[4] In rebuilding, the design has been modified to make it a neater and more business-like engine. The proportions of the chimney and the rectangular splasher have been improved and the semi-circular wheel splasher has been totally enclosed (the Ramsbottom version being perforated). The Webb additions can also be seen: the neat casing for the Ramsbottom safety valve, the long splasher for the coupling rod, and the cast-iron number plate (the latter introduced in 1878). All the elements of the early engines have been modified to produce an engine which has a modern appearance despite its small size.

Webb introduced cabs on the LNWR locomotives (where Ramsbottom had been satisfied with weatherboards). He explained that 'when he saw nine claims on the [LNWR Locomotive Insurance] society for deaths from consumption, he told the directors that the men must have better protection on the engines. He submitted to them the plan of his cab, and they at once adopted it.' [1]

The Webb cabs, or 'Dolly Vardens' as they were nicknamed [2], have been criticised, by latter-day writers, for providing too little protection – 'paltry' Hamilton Ellis called them.[3] The fact remains, however, that the drivers of the time preferred a small cab. In the 1860s drivers had complained when large cabs were introduced on the Great Eastern Railway [4] and on the Stockton & Darlington Railway.[5]

Similar complaints were made about Webb's cab, as was noted by Sir John Aspinall when he spoke to the Institution of Mechanical Engineers in 1925: 'I can well remember the time, about 1872, when Mr Webb put the first cab on to a LNW engine. As these cabs were added to other engines, much indignation was expressed by the drivers, who had from their daily exposure to the weather become very hardy, whereas when they worked on an engine with a cab they were kept much warmer while at work, but were much more affected by the weather on account of the changes of temperature when they were off the engine.' [6]

Other Webb innovations included the use of Joy's valve-gear, central bearings (made possible because Joy's valve-gear does not employ eccentrics), weighted wheel bosses, cast-iron wheel centres of H-section (introduced in 1872) [7], and tool boxes on the goods engines. The continuous splasher over the driving wheels, so characteristic of later LNWR engines, was introduced on the 'Bill Baileys'.

Those who see the passing of steam as the passing of the railways would have had no sympathy or support from F. W. Webb. At the annual prize-giving at the Crewe Mechanics' Institution in March 1896 he said he believed that 10 or 15 years hence they would have electric trains running to all the great centres at a speed which they then could hardly realise.[8]

He also spoke in favour of the use of electric traction in a discussion at the ICE in 1902 [9], and when his retirement was reported it was noted: 'that Mr Webb had in hand a complete and comprehensive scheme for the electrification of the LNWR in readiness for the time when it should be deemed expedient to adopt so vast and costly a change, and a plan had already been prepared by him for its application to some of the subur-

(1) Alexander McDonnell, a former pupil of Webb, had difficulties of this type on the North Eastern Railway. His designs were so unpopular among the drivers that he was forced to resign.
(2) *Railway Enthusiast's Guide* (2nd ed, 1962), p122: and also C. Hamilton Ellis, *British Railway History, 1830-1876*, p370.
(3) W. A. Tuplin, *North Western Steam*, p44.
(4) *Locomotives and Railways*, 7th March 1900 Vol 1. Facing p17 and photo on p18.

(1) Quoted CG, 27th April, 1934, p6.
(2) *ibid*
(3) C. Hamilton Ellis, *The South Western Railway*, p97.
(4) C. Hamilton Ellis, *Twenty Locomotive Men*, p38.
(5) *ibid*, p77-8.
(6) H. A. V. Bulleid, *Master Builders of Steam*, p50.
(7) *Locomotive Magazine*, Vol 15 (1909), p7.
(8) CC, 1st February 1896, p5.
(9) ICE, Vol 149 (1902), p112-5.

ban services.' [1] Webb was also interested in the motor car and shortly before his retirement had one built by the Maudslay Company at a cost of 900 guineas. [2]

Finally a note about tenders. Webb was rather scornful of the tender: 'the tendency of some engineers is to build their tenders as if they were very important pieces of machinery, spending a lot of money on them. He himself [Webb] has always looked upon them as water-carts, which should be built and hauled about as economically as possible.' [3] He also saw the tender as a shock absorber: 'Mr Webb believes that there should be a 'breaking piece' in all mechanism; this is, a piece that is sure to break first when a crash occurs from any possible cause. He makes his tenders the breaking piece in passenger engines.' [4] Thus the LNWR tender was a wooden framed, cheaply produced and standardised insurance policy.

(1) Quoted from *Page's Magazine* in *CG*, 3rd January 1903, p5.
(2) Quoted from *The Sketch* in *CG*, 4th April 1903, p4.
(3) C. J. Bowen Cooke, *On Recent Developments ...*, p62.
(4) *Locomotive Engineering*, (Dec 1892), p454: and see also C. Hamilton Ellis, *The Trains We Loved*, p123 on this topic.

General References - Books

Ahrons, E. L.
The British Steam Railway Locomotive, 1825-1925
Locomotive Publishing Co, 1927 (photo reprint 1960).
Fully indexed. The main source for technical details.
C. Hamilton Ellis says that 'this authority's summary of the Webb three-cylinder compounds, their advantages and disadvantages, in chapter 18 ... probably gives the most concise and at the same time the fairest summing up of their peculiarities yet written'.

Ahrons, E. L.
Locomotives and Train Working in the Latter Part of the Nineteenth Century, Vol 2 Heffer, 1952.
Pages 1 to 37 provide, in the words of Professor Simmons, 'perfunctory remarks on the LNW, which Ahrons (a loyal graduate of Swindon) disliked.' [1]

Cooke, C. J. Bowen
British Locomotives: their History, Construction, and Modern Development, Whittaker, 1893.
An authoritative book, written when Bowen Cooke was Outdoor Assistant, LNWR Locomotive Department. It is noted for its accuracy of detail.

Cooke, C. J. Bowen
Some Recent Developments in Locomotive Practice: an adaptation of two lectures delivered at the Royal Engineers' Institute, Chatham, Whittaker, 1902.
Supplements the above work.

Cotterell, S. and Wilkinson, G. H.
London & North-Western Locomotives, Simple and Compound, Holland Co, 1899.
Published in eight parts, at sixpence each, these little booklets contain some attractive photographs and a somewhat eccentric text.

Lake, Charles S.
The World's Locomotives Percival Marshall, (1905).
Most valuable for its illustrations. Chapter 9 concerns compound engines.

Livesey, H. F. F.
The Locomotives of the LNWR
Railway Publishing Co, 1948.
Important as it is a chronological account and contains a collection of good illustrations.

(1) *Journal of Transport History*, Vol 1 (1953), p63.

Maskelyne, J. N.
Locomotives I Have Known, Percival Marshall, 1959.
Drawings and notes on three Webb classes: the 'Jumbos' p88-9; the 'Watford Tanks' p90-1; and the 'Jubilees' , p92-3.

Maskelyne, J. N.
A Further Selection of Locomotives I Have Known
Percival Marshall, 1962.
Drawings and notes on: the 'Ladies of the Lake' [Webb's 1896 rebuilds] p 56-7; and the 'Cauliflowers' or 'Crested Goods' p58-9.

Montague, George.
Ten Years of Locomotive Progress, Alston Rivers, 1907.
Discusses locomotive development in the decade 1896-1906, a key period in Webb's career. It is useful particularly for its comparisons between the engines of the various companies. There is no index but the main references are:
p36-8
p51-3. Longer boilers. 'Greater Britain was the first express engine in this country fitted with a long boiler', p51. There is a table of boiler sizes, p52-3. 'In so far as [the adoption of the long boiler] for express passenger engines is concerned, the credit rests with Mr Webb, who was the first to conceive the idea of placing the four driving wheels in front of the fire-box', p55.
p59-60. Standardisation. Mr Montague does not give any credit to Rambottom or to Webb but suggests that standardisation came with Whale.
Chapter 5 is concerned with compounding, p105-25.
p107-8. Faults in Webb's compounds.
p106. LSWR trials – simples v. Webb compound.
p117-8. Webb's four-cylinder compounds.
p147-9. Webb's 0-8-0s: 'constituting ... at that time a new departure in locomotive practice ... These were the first engines ... to be fitted with the modern long boiler, and are therefore of unusual interest, while they were also the only three-cylinder compound engines in Great Britain'.
p146. Webb conversion of 0-8-0s into 2-8-0s.
p151. Webb's final design, the 4-6-0s.

Nock, O. S.
The Premier Line: the Story of the LNW Locomotives
Ian Allan, 1952.

Chapter 6, Webb – the first phase; chapter 7, Three-cylinder compounds; chapter 8, Webb – the last phase. A good general account giving lists of named engines and general information about the classes.

Poultney, Edward Cecil
British Express Locomotive Development, 1896-1948
Allen and Unwin, 1952.
Supplements Ahrons's *British Steam Railway Locomotive*, giving a technical analysis of the locomotives.
There is no index but the main references are:
Chapter 1 is mainly concerned with the LNWR locomotives used in the 1895 Railway Races. Full reference is made to *Hardwicke's* feat and the technical features of the 'Precedents' and the 'Precursors' are noted.
p37-9. *Iron Duke* as a four-cylinder simple.
p98-9,101-3. Webb's four-cylinder compounds.
p112-4. Boiler pressures: 'There seems no doubt that the higher pressures used by Webb for his compounds, attracted attention to the use of increased steam pressures ...' (p114).
p123-5. Return of the Webb approach with Bowen Cooke's designs.

Tuplin, W. A.
North Western Steam, Allen and Unwin, 1963.
A fresh assessment of the Crewe engine. Although the emphasis is on the Bowen Cooke period there is much that is new about Webb's locomotives.

General References - Periodical articles

Engineering, Vol 65 (1898), p20.
'Locomotive performances on the LNWR'
Table lists locomotive classes and gives running data.

Locomotive Engineer and Fireman's Journal, (1896), p100-110.
Littlejohn, B. H. 'LNWR locomotives, 1871-96'

North-Western Locomotive Journal, Vol.1-2, 1899.
An early junior railway enthusiasts' magazine entirely concerned with the LNWR. As it is a very slight publication, and as it appears to be a rarity – only the above volumes, now in the possession of the author, having been traced – no attempt has been made to analyse it.

Railway Engineer, Vol 18 (1897), p30-41.
Details of express engines: LNWR.
Illus. and text describing standard parts.

Railway Magazine, Vol 8 (1901), p360-6.
Lake, Charles S. 'The express locomotives of a great railway' [the LNWR]. Well illustrated article.

Railway Magazine, Vol 19 (1906), p118-26.
'The Diamond Jubilee of the LNWR: the locomotives'

Railway Magazine, Vol 32 (1913), p500-2.
Coe, Reginald H. 'The tank engines of a great railway'
Includes notes on the Webb engines running in 1913.

Railway Magazine, Vol 36 (1915), p17-24,135-42, 221-7, 373-83. Ahrons, E. L. 'Locomotive and train working in the latter part of the nineteenth century: LNWR'
Articles reprinted in book form but with different photographs.

Railway Magazine, Vol 79 (1936), p113-20.
Nock, O. S. 'The locomotives of the LNWR, 1897-1922: Part 1, 1897-1902'
Part 2 of this article, (p186-95) covering the years 1903-1909, also describes the fate of some of Webb's engines in the period that Whale was CME.

Railway Magazine, Vol 88 (1942), p 328-9.
Walton, W. M. 'F. W. Webb's simple engines'

References to Classes of Locomotives

Crewe Works 0-4-0 Tramway Engines
Two 18in-gauge locomotives, similar to five built by Ramsbottom, *Dickie* built 1872 and *Billy* built 1875.

Engineering, Vol 20 (1875), p228-9.
Description of a visit to Crewe Works by the Iron and Steel Institute. Includes a description of *Billy*.

Engineering, Vol 22 (1876), p174, (illus p178).
'Locomotives for the 18in gauge railway at Crewe'

Railway Magazine, Vol 18 (1906), p130-6.
Gairns, J. F. 'Some curious British locomotives'
Includes a description of *Billy*.

SLS, Vol 27 (1952), p305, (photo p304).
'The Crewe Works footbridge'
A description of the tramway. The photo shows Ramsbottom's *Midge* on the footbridge.

17in 0-6-0 Coal Engine
Class of 500 engines built 1873 to 1892.

Locomotive Magazine, Vol 15 (1909), p35-6.
A Great Western Railway goods engine built at Crewe. A curiosity in the form of an 0-6-0 coal engine with GWR tender and smoke-box door. It was formerly owned by the Manchester & Milford Railway and was absorbed into the GWR.

LRCWR, Vol 60 (1954), p4.
'The Last LNWR Webb 'coal' engine'
Brief news item with details and period photograph.

LRCWR, Vol 60 (1954), p152.
Cope, R. K. 'Last LNWR 0-6-0 coal engine'
Photo. And post-Webb history of some of the survivors.

Locomotives and Railways, Vol 3 (1902), p90.
'LNWR Six-Coupled Coal Engines'

Railway Magazine, Vol 90 (1944), p225.
'Two Famous LNWR Classes'
Also describes the 'Cauliflowers'.

SLS, Vol 27 (1951), p159-60.
'A Note on the Webb coal engines'
Line illustrations with list of survivors.

**The 'Precedent' and 'Improved Precedent' 2-4-0s -
'The Jumbos' or 'Large Jumbos'**
Class of 166 named engines, 70 of which were originally 'Precedents' built 1874-1882, and 96 'Newtons' built by Ramsbottom, all rebuilt by Webb as 'Improved Precedents' in 1887-1901.

Fenton, E. W.
Locomotives in Retirement, Hugh Evelyn, 1958.
A coloured plate of *Hardwicke* with a page of descriptive notes and a brief character study of Webb. The plate caption gives the technical details.

Nock, O. S.
Historical Steam Locomotives, A. and C. Black, 1959.
Chapter 5: The North-Western 'Jumbos'.

Locomotive Magazine, Vol 7 (1902) p168.
The *Charles Dickens*, LNWR.
Illustration and description of 'the most famous engine of a famous class'.

Locomotives and Railways, Vol 1 (1900), p17-20, 37, 40-2, 54-6.
Brewer, F. W., 'The NW Precedents'

Railway Engineer, Vol 13 (1892), p291-2.
'Express passenger engine, *Charles Dickens*, LNWR'
Plate and full details.

Railway Magazine, Vol 4 (1899), p206-12, 370-5.
Rous-Marten, Charles, 'Some Wonderful Little Engines'

Railway Magazine, Vol 31 (1912), p211-6.
Coe, Reginald H.,
'Precedent LNW four-coupled locomotives'

Railway Magazine, Vol 70 (1932), p349-51.
Nock, O. S., 'The Passing of the Jumbos'

Railway Magazine, Vol 76 (1935), p79-81.
Hewitt, F. and Nock, O. S., 'The LNWR Jumbo types'

The 'Precursor' 2-4-0s
Class of 40 named engines built 1874 to 1879.

Engineering, Vol 19 (1875), p185-6.
'Passenger Locomotive for the LNWR'
Full description with illustrations

Locomotive Magazine, Vol 8 (1903) p 94-5.
'The Precursor class, LNWR'

4ft 6in 2-4-0 'Chopper' tank engine
Class of 50 engines built 1876-1880: 40 were later converted to 2-4-2 tanks and some converted back again.

Engineering, Vol 24 (1877), p436,473.
'Tank locomotive for the LNWR'
Full description with illus.

SLS, Vol 28 (1952), p272-3 (photo. p267)
'The LNWR 2-4-0 tanks'
Brief details and full list of numbers with dates built, etc.

4ft 6in 2-4-2 tank engine
Class of 180 engines built 1879-1890.

18in Goods 0-6-0: 'The Cauliflowers' or 'Crested Goods'
A class of 310 engines built 1880-1902.

Engineering, Vol 30 (1880), p294-6, (illus. facing p298).
'Goods Locomotive: LNWR'
Full details. There is a further description in Vol 31 (1881), p92-3.

LRCWR, Vol 50 (1944), p22.
Hambleton, F. C.
'The first locomotive to be fitted with Joy's valve gear'

Railway Magazine, Vol 90 (1944), p 225.
'Two famous LNWR classes'
Also describes the 17in 0-6-0 Coal Engine.

SLS, Vol 24 (1948), p 310-11.
Gradon, W. McGowan, The LNWR 'Cauliflowers'.
Line illustrations and description.

SLS, Vol 26 (1950), p252-3.
LNWR the 'Crested' goods.
With list of survivors, numbers dates built, etc.

SLS, Vol 27 (1951), p159-60.
'A Note on the Webb Coal Engine'
Line illustrations with list of survivors.

Small 0-4-0 small shunting engine
Class of 10 standard gauge engines built 1880-1882.

Engineer, Vol 82 (1896), p 297.
'Oil burning locomotive, Liverpool Docks'
Includes an illus. of No. 3017.

Engineering, Vol 30 (1880), p191, (illus. p184).
'Shunting Engine: LNWR'
Full details.

Engineering, Vol 62 (1896), p251.
Oil-burning locomotive for the Liverpool Dock lines.

4ft 0-4-2 Crane Shunter
Class of 3 crane shunting enghines built in 1892.

Locomotive Magazine, Vol 5 (1900), p24.
Four-coupled shunting engine, LNWR.

Special DX 0-6-0 goods engine
500 rebuilt 1881-1890.

Locomotive Magazine, Vol 4 (1899), p169-70.
'The DX goods engines, LNWR'
Details of Webb's rebuilds.

LRCWR, vol37 (1931), p 3.
'DX goods engines, LNWR'
Includes details of Webb's rebuilds.

0-6-2 Coal Tank engine: 'Mourners' or 'Gadgets'
Class of 300 engines built 1881 to 1890.[1]

SLS, Vol 32 (1956), p140-1.
'The Webb side tank coal engines'
Gives list of numbers.

Trains Illustrated, Vol 8 (1955), p112-13, (Letters p219).
McNaught, R. S., 'Memories of the Coal Tanks'

The Compound Locomotives, 1882-1905
Acworth, W. M., *The Railways of England*
John Murray, 5th ed, 1900 (photo reprint Ian Allan, 1963).
Chapter 2 discusses the compounds.

Dearden, G. A.
'Observations on the 'Teutonics', 'Greater Britains', and four-cylinder compounds, LNWR'
Holland Co, Birmingham, (1899).
A defence of the compounds in the form of a 14 page pamphlet. There is a copy in the British Museum.

Engineering, Vol 57 (1894), p610-11.
'The Webb system of compounding locomotives'
Includes a double-page illus.: 'The development of the Webb system of compounding locomotives'.

Feilden's Magazine, Vol 2 (1900), p365-76, 485-93.
Rous-Marten, Charles
'Compound and four-cylinder locomotives in England and France'

Feilden's Magazine, Vol 7 (1902), p420-32.
Lake, Charles S.
'Modern compound locomotives: section 1, English and French locomotives (Webb and De Glehn system)'

ICE, Vol 139 (1900), p308-17.
Wolff, C. E.
'The relative advantages of ordinary and compound engines'
The Webb three-cylinder compounds are considered on

(1) *Trains Illustrated*, Vol 6 (1953), p196.

pages 314-5, and the four-cylinder compounds on pages 315-6.

LRCWR, Vol 42 (1936), p287-9, (Letters p335, 368, 402-3 and Vol 43 (1937), p63.
Smith, Ernest F.
'The Webb three-cylinder compounds: their supposed automatic crank adjustment'

LRCWR, Vol 56 (1950), p93-4, 143, 202.
Correspondence concerning Webb's three-cylinder compounds.
'The great number of letters received on this subject compels us to condense correspondence ...' (p202).

Locomotives and Railways, Vol 3 (1902), p24-7, 57-8, 107-8.
Vol 4 (1903), p61-2. (No other parts traced).
'The NW compound locomotives'

Railroad Gazette, Vol 21 (1889), p257-9.
'Compound locomotives'
During the discussion the President of the New England Railroad Club reads extracts from some of Webb's letters.

Railway Engineer, Vol 19 (1898), p35.
Compound engines, on the LNWR.
Running details.

Railway Magazine, Vol 8 (1901), p454-61, Vol 9 (1901), p97-104.
Rous-Marten, Charles
'What Mr Webb's compounds have done.'

Railway Magazine, Vol 61 (1927), p458-9.
LNWR three-cylinder compound express locomotives.
'Several readers have indicated interest in the now almost-forgotten three-cylinder compound locomotives designed by Mr F. W. Webb ...'.
Lists with brief details, which are of little value, but it would be interesting to know what stimulated the curiosity about the compounds in 1927.

Railway Magazine, Vol 102 (1956), p511-16,523, 786.
'Mercury'
'The LNWR Webb three-cylinder compound locomotives'
Were the compounds a failure or not? The controversy continues.

SLS, Vol 26 (1950), p 254-6.
Kalla-Bishop, P. M., 'Triple-expansion compounds'
There are line illustrations of the Allan 2-2-2 as a two-cylinder compound (No. 1874) and as a three-cylinder compound (No. 3088).

Trains Illustrated, No. 1 (1946), p18-22, No. 3 (1946), p13-18, No. 6 (1947), p14-15, No. 8 (1947), p11-13.
Bucknall, Rixon, 'The Webb compounds: their conception, evolution and failure'

'Experiment' 2-2-2-0 Passenger Engine
Class of 30 named three-cylinder compounds built 1882-1884.

Engineer, Vol 53 (1882), p163.
Compound locomotive, LNWR: ('Experiment').
Illustrations and text.

LRCWR, Vol 43 (1937), p60-1.
Hambleton, F. C.,
LNWR compounds: the Experiment' class.

Railway Engineer, Vol 3 (1882), p78.
Webb's three-cylinder compound *Experiment*.
Plate and details.

Railway Engineer, Vol 3 (1882), p285.
'Webb's three-cylinder compound locomotive'
Drawings and text by Webb.

'Dreadnought' 2-2-2-0 Passenger Engine
Class of 40 named three-cylinder compounds built 1884-1888.

Engineer, Vol 59 (1885), p349, 352.
The Invention Exhibition – compound locomotive, LNWR.
Illustrations and text describing *Marchioness of Stafford*.

Engineer, Vol 66 (1888), p511, 515.
Compound locomotives on the LNWR: [*Marchioness of Stafford*].
'The engraving is ... the largest that has ever been published of a locomotive engine'.

Engineering, Vol 39 (185), p462-72, (illustrations p 59).
'Compound passenger locomotive' [*Dreadnought*].
Illustrations and full details.

LRCWR, Vol 43 (1937), p 162-3.
Hambleton, F. C.
LNWR compounds: the 'Dreadnought' class.

Railroad Gazette, (21.8.1885).
'The Compound Locomotive *Dreadnought*.'
Full description with illustrations and diagrams.

The Compound Tank Engines
Four engines built 1884-1887:
'Metropolitan' 4-2-2-0 tank rebuilt as compound in 1884, No. 2063; 2-2-2-2 tank No. 687 built in 1885; 2-2-2-2 tank No. 600, the 3000th engine built at Crewe, in 1887; and 2-2-4-0 tank No. 777, built in 1887.

Engineering, Vol 39 (1885), p462-72, (illustrations p 458).
'Compound tank locomotive' ('Metropolitan' engine).
Full details.

Engineering, Vol 44 (1887), p13, 649.
'Compound tank locomotive at the Manchester Exhibition' (No. 777).

LRCWR, Vol 43 (1937), p298-300.
Hambleton, F. C.,
'LNWR compounds: the four side tanks'

LRCWR, Vol 48 (1942), p176-7.
Hambleton, F. C.
LNW compounds: 'Metropolitan', 5ft 6in Tank, and *Triplex* classes.

Railroad Gazette, Vol 19 (1887), p614-15.
'Compound tank locomotive (Webb's patent), LNWR' (No. 687).

Railway Magazine, Vol 19 (1906), p238.
'LNWR three-cylinder compound tank engine No. 2974' (No. 777).
Illustrations and details.

Railway Magazine, Vol 87 (1941), p334-5, 471.
'Webb compound tanks, LNWR'

'Teutonic' 2-2-2-0 Passenger Engine
Class of 10 named three-cylinder compounds built 1889-1890.

Engineer, Vol 68 (1889), p143, (plate between p 140-1).
'Compound locomotive, LNWR' (*Oceanic*).

Engineering, Vol 47 (1889), p601, 656.
'Compound passenger locomotive: *Teutonic*'
Page 656 gives details of the valve-gear.

Engineering, Vol 50 (1890), p98-100.
'Compound locomotive for the LNWR: Edinburgh Exhibition'
Illus. and full details of *Jeanie Deans*.

LRCWR, Vol 44 (1938), p89-90, (letters p402 and Vol 45 (1939), p30,93).
Hambleton, F. C.,
'LNW compounds: the 'Teutonic' class'

Railway Engineer, Vol 18 (1897), p34.
'The Webb compound engine *Jeanie Deans* No. 1304'
Running details.

Railway Engineer, Vol 21 (1900), p1.
'Webb's compound engine *Jeanie Deans*: LNWR'
Running details.

The 'Whitworth' or 'Small Jumbo' 2-4-0s
Class of 90 engines built in 1889 to 1896. They took the names and numbers of the 'Samsons' and were identical to the other 'Jumbos' except that they had smaller driving wheels – 6ft instead of 6ft 6in – and a longer wheel-base.

Railway Magazine, Vol 44 (1919), p43-8.
Alcock, C. J., 'A famous 'dual-identity' locomotive class' ('Samson'/'Whitworth' class).

'910' 2-4-2 Tank Engines
Class of 160 simple engines built 1890-1897, including 40 converted from 2-4-0 'Precursors'.

LRCWR, Vol 62 (1956), p18.
'LNWR Webb 2-4-2 Tank.'
Photograph, details and brief news item: 'Locomotive No. 46616, 66 years old veteran, and last of the LNWR 5ft 6in side tank passenger class of engines, is now at Crewe for breaking up'.

Railway World, Vol 16 (1955), p19-21.
McNaught, R. S., 'The last Webb 2-4-2 tanks'

SLS, Vol 30 (1954), p19-20, (photograph p1).
'A Note on the Webb 5ft 6in 2-4-2 tank engines'
List of the engines handed over to British Railways, with dates of building and other details.

'Greater Britain' 2-2-2-2 Passenger Engine
Class of ten three-cylinder compounds built 1891-1894.

Engineer, Vol 72 (1891), p425 (plate p421).
'Compound express locmotive LNWR' [*Greater Britain*]

Engineer, Vol 76 (1893), p191.
Rous-Marten, Charles
'A Remarkable Locomotive' [*Greater Britain*]
Includes diagrams

Engineering, Vol 52 (1891), p565-6.
'The Compound Locomotive *Greater Britain*'
Illustrations and full details.

Engineering, Vol 56 (1893), p110-111.
'The Compound Locomotive *Greater Britain*'
Running details.

LRCWR, Vol 44 (1938), p217.
Hambleton, F. C.
'LNWR Compounds: the "Greater Britain" class'

Railway Engineer, Vol 12 (1891), p309-11.
'Eight-wheeled Compound (F. W. Webb's System) Engine, *Greater Britain*, LNWR'
Plate and remarkably full details.

Railway Engineer, Vol 20 (1899), p202.
'Performance of Webb Compound Engines of "Greater Britain" class LNWR'

Railway Magazine, Vol 10 (1902), p363-8
'Brunel Redivivus'
A LNWR locomotive and rolling stock in the United States.
Full description of *Queen Empress*, including the combustion chamber and its 'steam blast apparatus for cleaning the soot out of the tubes'.

Railway Magazine, Vol 90 (1944), p151-2.
'A Remarkable Webb Compound Performance'
Greater Britain under test in April 1893 ran 3,612 miles in six days with an average coal consumption of 29.87lb per mile.

Eight-coupled Goods and Mineral Engines
A simple 0-8-0 engine, No. 2524, was built in 1892. It was followed by a class of 111 three-cylinder componds, class A, built in 1893-1900, and by 170 four-cylinder compounds, class B, built in 1901-1904.

Gregory, J. R., *The LNWR Eight-coupled Goods Engines*
Railway Correspondence and Travel Society, 1950.

IMechE, 1894, p458-61.
Brief description of a visit by the IMechE to Crewe Works.
Details are given of the comparative tests between the two 0-8-0 locomotives, No. 50 (compound) and No. 2524 (simple) on 1st April. The results of the tests are tabulated on p460.

Railway Magazine, Vol 10 (1902), p543-9.
Poultney, Edward Cecil.
'Some modern British goods and mineral locomotives'
Includes discussion and illustrations of the Webb 0-8-0 engines.

Eight-coupled Goods Engine
One simple engine, No. 2524, built 1892.

Engineer, Vol 74 (1892), p565, (illustrations p560).
'Eight-wheeled coupled goods engine'

Engineering, Vol 54 (1892), p780, (illustrations p775).
'Eight-wheeled coupled locomotive for mineral traffic'

Locomotive Magazine, Vol 9 (1903), p261.
'No. 2524, LNWR'
Details and line illustrations.

Metropolitan-type 4-4-2 Tank Engine
Ten engines rebuilt from 4-4-0 tank engines between May and December 1892.

0-4-2ST Crane Shunter
Class of 8 engines built 1892-5.
Railway Magazine, Vol 97 (1951), p661, (photo p665).
Casserley, H. C., 'Crane engines'
There is also a letter referring to this class in Vol 98 (1952), p137-8.

Class 'A' eight-coupled Goods Engine
Class of 111 three-cylinder compound engines built 1893-1900.
Locomotive Magazine, Vol 2 (1897), p26.
'Eight-coupled goods engine for the LNWR'
Illustrations and full details.

Locomotive Magazine, Vol 4 (1899), p123.
'Eight-coupled compound mineral engine, LNWR'
Illustrations and text.

LRCWR, Vol 44 (1938), p325-7.
Hambleton, F. C.
'LNW compounds: the three-cylinder mineral engines'

'John Hick' 2-2-2-2 passenger engine
Class of 10 named three-cylinder compounds built 1894-8.

LRCWR, Vol 46 (2940), p36-7.
Hambleton, F.C.
Webb compounds; 'John Hick' class, LNWR.

Renewed 'Lady of the Lake' or 'Problem' 2-2-2 passenger engine
Virtually new engines but described as rebuilds of Ramsbottom's engines. This 'class' appeared in 1895-7.

Engineer, Vol 82 (1896), p662, (illustrations p658)
Outside-cylinder passenger engines, LNWR.

Engineer, Vol 83 (1897), p396, (drawing p392).
Express passenger engine, LNWR.

Locomotives and Railways, Vol 1 (1900), p142-5.
Mr J. Ramsbottom's 'Lady of the Lake' class, LNWR.

SLS, Vol 28 (1952), p 38-40, (illus. p56).
Rollason, M. H., 'The LNWR Problems, 1859-1907.'

0-4-2ST Dock Shunter
Class of 20 engines built 1896-1901.

Locomotive Magazine, Vol 5 (1900), p24.
Four-coupled shunting engine, LNWR.

SLS, Vol 27 (1951), p259-60.
'Box tanks.'

SLS, Vol 32 (1956), p353.
'The Last of the LNWR 'Bissel' tanks.'

'Jubilee' 4-4-0 passenger engine
Class of 40 named four-cylinder compounds built 1897-1900.

Engineer, Vol 85 (1898), p420-1.
Four-cylinder compound passenger engine.
Illustrations, drawings and details of Black Prince.

Engineering, Vol 64 (1897), p693-4, (illustrations facing p684).
Four-cylinder compound locomotive.
Full details of Black Prince.
Engineering, Vol 65 (1898), p239.
'Four-cylinder coupled compound locomotive Black Prince.' Illustrations and brief text.

Feilden's Magazine, Vol 5 (1901), p111-24.
Horsfall, Jas.,
'A bit of locomotive practice of the LNWR.'
Article about Black Prince.

Locomotive Magazine, Vol 2 (1897), p147.
'Four-cylinder compound bogie express engine, LNWR.'
Illustrations and text describing Black Prince.

Locomotive Magazine, Vol 4 (1899), p76.
'Our coloured supplement: four-cylinder compound express engine, LNWR.'
Illustrations and text describing Jubilee.

LRCWR, Vol 47 (1941), p38-9.
Hambleton, F. C.
'LNWR compounds: the Black Prince class.'

Railroad Gazette, Vol 30 (1898), p115, 277.
'Compound passenger locomotive, LNWR.'
Black Prince.

Railway Engineer, Vol 19 (1898), p6-7, 66.
'7ft 0in four wheels coupled four-cylinder compound passenger engine Black Prince: LNWR.'
Drawings and full details.

Railway Engineer, Vol 20 (1899), p203-4, 234-5, 270.
'A Great Locomotive Performance: LNWR.'
Iron Duke carries ICE members to Crewe.

Railway Magazine, Vol 5 (1899), p192.
'Our coloured plate: Mr Webb's four-wheels coupled compound passenger locomotive Black Prince.'
Full details.

Radial 0-6-2 passenger tank engine: 'Watford Tanks'
Class of 80 engines built 1898-1902.

Engineer, Vol 87 (1899), p497, (illustrations p489).
Side tank passenger engine.
Brief text giving details.

Locomotive Magazine, Vol 3 (1898), p169.
Six-coupled passenger tank engine, LNWR.
Illustrations and full details.

Railway World, Vol 16 (1955), p126-9.
Tuplin, W. A., 'Webb's Watford Tanks'

'Alfred the Great' 4-4-0 passenger engine
Class of 40 named four-cylinder compounds built 1901-1904.

Locomotive Magazine, Vol 6 (1901), p147.
'New four-cylinder compound express engines, LNWR'
Short text and illustrations of Edward VII.
LRCWR, Vol 47 (1941), p85-6.

Hambleton, F. C.
'LNWR compounds: the "King Alfred" class'

Railway Engineer, Vol 22 (1901), p262-3.
'Four-cylinder compound (Webb's system) "Alfred the Great" class express engines: LNWR'
Plate and details.

Class 'B' eight-coupled Goods Engine: 'Swamis', 'Piano fronts' and 'Foggy nights'.[1]
Class of 170 four-cylinder compounds built 1901-1904.

Engineer, Vol 94 (1902), p66, (illustrations p62).
'Mineral locomotive, LNWR'
Short text giving details.

Locomotive Magazine, Vol 7 (1902), p35.
'Eight-coupled four-cylinder compound coal engine, LNWR.'
Illustrations and details.

LRCWR, Vol 48 (1942), p47.
Hambleton, F. C.
'LNW compounds: the "B" class mineral engines'

Locomotives and Railways, Vol 3 (1902), p47-8.
'4ft 3in 8-coupled 4-cylinder compound mineral locomotive, LNWR'

Railway Engineer, Vol 23 (1902), p270-1.
'8-coupled 4-cylinder compound mineral locomotive: LNWR'

'1400' mixed-traffic 4-6-0 engine, the 'Bill Baileys'
Class of 30 four-cylinder compounds built 1903-1905.

Engineer, Vol 95 (1903), p542.
'Six-wheel coupled compound goods engine, LNWR'
Photo. And brief text giving details.

Locomotive Magazine, Vol 8 (1903), p334.
'New six-coupled mixed traffic locomotive, LNWR'

LRCWR, Vol 48 (1942), p146.
Hambleton, F.C.,
'LNW compounds: the mixed traffic engine'

Railway Magazine, Vol 12 (1903), p478.
'Mr F. W. Webb's last locomotive design'
Illustrations and full details.

Compounds for Foreign Railways

General.

LRCWR, Vol 39 (1933), p332-5.
Vivian, H.
Webb compound locomotives on foreign railways.
Argentina.
In 1885 one compound locomotive, named *Mariano Haedo*, was built by Messrs. Dübs and Co.

Austria.
In 1884 one compound, *Combermere*, was built by Messrs Sharp, Stewart & Co.

(1) W. A. Tuplin. *North Western Steam*, p88, 91.

Brazil.
In 1885 one compound, *Dr. F. N. Prates,* was built by Messrs Sharp, Stewart & Co for the Paulista Railway.

Engineer, Vol 60 (1885), p283, (illustrations p280, diagrams between p338-9).
'Compound locomotive, Webb's patent, for the Companhia Paulista.'

Engineering, Vol 40 (1885), p610, 614.
'Compound locomotive, Webb's system, for the Paulista Railway, Brazil.'

Canada.
In 1884 a 4-2-2-0 compound express engine was designed for the Grand Trunk Railroad. The drawings are still at Crewe Works, but it is doubtful if this locomotive was ever built.

Chile.
In 1884 two 4-2-4-2 side tank compounds were built by Robert Stephenson & Co for the Antofagasta Railway, 2ft 6in gauge.
There is a brief mention in Ahrons, *BSRL*, p321.

France.
In 1884 one engine, *Compound*, was built by Messrs Sharp, Stewart & Co for the Western Railway.

India.
In 1884 the Oudh & Rohilkund Railway bought 10 Webb compounds which were built by Messrs. Dübs & Co. There is a brief mention in Ahrons, *BSRL*, p327.

United States of America.
In 1889 one engine, *Pennsylvania*, was built by Messrs. Beyer, Peacock & Co for the Pennsylvania Railroad.

Railroad Gazette, Vol 21 (1889), p288-9, (editorial comment p44-5).
'The *Pennsylvania* compound locomotive'
There is also a description of a ride on *Pennsylvania*, p199.

Railway Age, (1.3.1889).
'The Pennsylvania's English locomotive'
This is little more than an explanation of Webb's system of compounding.

Railway Age, (22.3.1889).
The Pennsylvania's English engine criticised by the engineer. The opinions are those of Alexander Pitcairn, engineer of the Pennsylvania Railroad Company.

Railway Magazine, Vol 23 (1908), p244-5.
A Webb compound on the Pennsylvania Railroad.

2d - Crewe Works

Much attention has been given to Webb as a locomotive designer but his contribution to the development of Crewe Works has been neglected. This is perhaps inevitable: the history of the locomotives is relatively easy to trace and it is attractive to read. In contrast great labour would be required in order to gather sufficient material for a history of the works, and, although it would reveal Webb's greatest contributions to engineering, it would be of interest only to readers of industrial history.

The general growth of the works can be gauged in terms of acreage and numbers of employees. Isolated production figures can also be found which reflect the scale of output: in 1872, for example, 146 locomotives were produced [1], Acworth tells us that in the 1880s 'Crewe every five days withdraws a worn out engine and replaces it by a new one' [2] and Charlie Dick says that 'lately [1886] we have been building about 70 a year, but for some years we did about 110 and one year 140.' [3] Crewe was too successful at engine building, for in March 1876 the private manufacturers of locomotives obtained and served on the LNWR an injunction restraining it from producing engines or rolling stock except for its own use.[4]

Locomotives were only one manufacture at Crewe, however. The works produced all its own steel and used it to roll its own rails [5] and plates for the Dublin and Holyhead passenger boats, and to make boilers for the locomotives and vessels: in the twenty years 1875 to 1896 4,000 Bessemer steel boilers were made [6] and in 1895 annual production was given as 200 boilers with repairs to a further 2,700.[7] From 1874 all signalling equipment was made at Crewe.[8] Crewe even produced its own bricks ('We make on an average 300,000 red bricks per week, and have done so for years' [9]) and soap.

Webb was fond of 'stunts' which would demonstrate the efficiency of the works. In 1878, for example, he showed that an engine could be assembled in 25½ hours.[10] This was an artificial display of efficiency, but the collapse of the Llandulas Viaduct in 1879 was an opportunity to show that steel could be made and rolled into 42 girders, each 32 feet long, in seven days.[11]

Although Webb's locomotive policy had failed by the time of his retirement, he had so developed the works that his successor, George Whale, was able to correct the situation by turning out 365 locomotives of new designs in five years.[1]

To trace the process of developing production and efficiency, to show the expansion of the works in more detail, is a difficult task. The works records were destroyed about 1960 and so this important source is lost. There are, however, various references to plant and processes scattered through books and periodicals. D. L. Burn mentions the introduction, in 1876, of a three-high mill using a Corliss engine [2], Webb's curvilinear slotting machine was mentioned in various places [3], and J. G. B. Sams has recorded that during his period at the works (1897-1902) the Bessemer process was replaced by the Siemens-Martin Open Hearth system, and the heavy, horizontal hammers ('that always reminded me of rams fighting') were replaced by hydraulic forging presses.[4] Many of Webb's processes are described in the proceedings of the engineering institutions, as the curvilinear slotting machine mentioned above, and his method of casting wheels in a revolving mould.[5]

In order to systematically show the development of the factory it would be necessary to work through the Minutes of the Locomotive Committee in which purchase of all new tools, from a 30-ton Duplex Hammer to such things as lathes, had to be approved. Analysis of the various accounts of visits to the works would also be necessary to find mention of new processes and machines. Photographs which illustrate these accounts might also be examined.

One good account of life in the works deserves mention, J. G. B. Sams's record of the years 1897 to 1902. In his articles we have a record of the changes taking place in the works during Webb's time:

'At the end of this period [1897-1902] I was moved into No. 8 Shop at the Steel Works, on new construction. Here I found three systems in force that have since become to a great extent standards in engineering practice. In No. 4 Erecting Shop a gang of men under a leading hand built one engine throughout from the frames, which were all put together by a specialist gang, and there were about ten new-work pits, each building an engine. But in No. 8 Shop, each pair of erectors, or an erector and apprentice, took a certain part of the engine, and worked at that only on every engine as it was built, rapidly becoming specialists, the advantage being that by specialising the men did their parts better and quicker, and only needed the tools for their own particular jobs.

(1) C. E. R. Sherrington. *A Hundred Years of Inland Transport*, p220, and Steel, p341.
(2) W. M. Acworth *The Railways of England*, p72.
(3) Peter Taylor *Autobiography*, p184-5
(4) Between 1871 and 1874 a hundred and one locomotives were built for the L&YR: all to the designs of Ramsbottom: see *Locomotive Magazine*, Vol 8 (1903), p358.
(5) Monthly production figures for rails are given, in tons, in the Minutes of the LNWR Locomotive Committee.
(6) Sir Henry Bessemer, *An Autobiography*, p255.
(7) LNWR. *Visit of the International Congress ...*
(8) *Railway Magazine*, Vol 5 (1899), p238.
(9) Peter Taylor, *ibid*, p185.
(10) Chaloner. p73; *Railroad Gazette* for 28.9.1888.
(11) G. P. Neale, *Railway Reminiscences*, p237; *Cassier's Magazine*, Vol 10 (1896), p133-4; Steel, p375-7; George Findlay, *Working ...*, p62-3, and most of the obituaries.

(1) O. S. Nock, *The Premier Line*, p151.
(2) D. L. Burn, *The Economic History of Steelmaking* (1940), p60.
(3) *Engineering*, Vol 17 (1874), p30; *IMechE*, 1866, p280-7.
(4) *Railway Magazine*, Vol 54 (1924), p385.
(5) *ICE*, Vol 73 (1883) p99-101.

'The next point was that the engines were built to spirit-level and jigs, and the cylinders, motion plates, etc., set to lines scribed along the frames, and not to piano-wire lines set up through centres, the advantage here being a more standard engine owing to the greater accuracy all round. The last point was that the frames were laid down at one end of the shop by the identical leading hand (Teddy Battams) from No. 4 Shop, and as construction on them progressed, the engines were moved down the shop towards the exit, the final coupling-up and valve setting taking place on the end pits of all. This system is very largely used in motor-car and lorry construction today, the difference being that in the latter case the units under construction are moved forward on a slow-moving platform, while the Crewe method was to lift the engines further along the shop as required by overhead cranes.' [1]

If such detailed accounts were more common, the task of the historian would be much easier. Unfortunately, there appears to be only one giving a similar amount of detail and that is to be found in an American periodical.[2]

Labour relations at Crewe were as bad as they were on the rest of the railways. Anti-unionism was common among the senior officials of the Company. The Chairman, Richard Moon, had no time for unions, and 'for thirty years ... commanded, dominated and oppressed the LNWR Board, its officers, its officials, its every member down to junior porters and van boys' [3], while General Manager George Findlay's attitude is expressed in his statement 'that you might as well have trade unionism in Her Majesty's Army as to have it in the railway service. The thing is totally incompatible.' [4]

Although Webb was prepared to negotiate on occasion, as in the discussion on the nine-hour day,[5] he always supported the views of the Chairman and General Manager. When the first Crewe Branch of the Amalgamated Society of Railway Servants was established 'about June, 1888' action was soon taken. Its first secretary, J. Unsworth, resigned after ten months, having been 'had up in the office' by his rail chief for Trade Union activity.[6]

Matters came to a head in December, 1896, when Frederick Harrison, Findlay's successor, dismissed a large number of ASRS members (who were re-instated after a great public outcry). By this time Webb had learned the lessons of the 'Intimidation Affair' (fully discussed in Section 2e) and even the hostile *Crewe Chronicle* had to admit that Webb was not in any way responsible.[7]

(1) *Railway Magazine*, Vol 54 (1924), p382-3.
(2) *Locomotive Engineering*, (Dec 1892), p449, 451, 453, 455.
(3) C. Hamilton Ellis, *British Railway History, 1877-1947*, p17.
(4) Royal Commission on Labour, BPP 1893-4, Vol 33, Q 25945, quoted in P. S. Bagwell, *The Railwaymen*, p96.
(5) *CG*, 25th November, 1871, p5.
(6) NUR. *Official souvenir of the annual general meeting of delegates ... 1923, at ... Crewe*, p8.
(7) *CC*, 12th December, 1896, p8.

2d - Descriptions of Crewe Works

LRCWR, Vol 49 (1945), p152-4.
'Crewe Centenary'
Includes some useful details about Crewe Works in Webb's time.

1872
Engineering, Vol 14 (1872), p94-5.
Description of a visit by the Institution of Mechanical Engineers. Tour conducted by Webb.

1873
Nasir-al-Din, Shah of Persia.
The Diary of H. M. the Shah of Persia, during his tour through Europe in A. D. 1873, John Murray, 1874.
An account of the Shah's visit to the works is given on pages 182 to 183. It is little more than a curiosity. This visit was also reported in the *Illustrated London News*, Vol 63 (1873), p19, and there is a badly drawn picture of the Shah watching the Bessemer process on p13.

1875
Engineering, Vol 20 (1875), p228-9.
Description of a visit by the Iron and Steel Institute. Tour conducted by Webb.

1879
Engineering, Vol 28 (1879), p264-6.
Illustrations p260-1.
Description of a visit by the Iron and Steel Institute. There are illustrations of machine tools. This visit was also reported in *ISI*, 1879, p631-3.

1882
Engineer, Vol 53 (1882), p284.
Tour of the 'new foundry' by Manchester Association of Employers and Foremen.

1884
Engineer, Vol 58 (1884), p263.
Description of a visit by the Iron and Steel Institute. Tour conducted by Webb.
An interesting account as it is rather critical of Crewe finish and the use of out-dated tools.
This visit is also reported in *Engineering*, Vol 38 (1884), p309-11.

1886
Taylor, Peter, *Autobiography*. Alexander Gardner (Paisley), Cheaper edition, 1917.
Chapter XI consists of two letters from Charlie Dick, the second of which, dated 13th October, 1886, gives a useful description of the Works.

1889
Engineer, Vol 67 (1889), p498-500.
Brief description of tour by party of American engineers.

1880s
Acworth, W. M., *The Railways of England*. John Murray, 5th ed, 1900.
The works is described in Chapter 2. The illustrations include a good picture of the rail mill (facing p67).

Findlay, George, *The Working and Management of an English Railway*. Whittaker, 1889.
The General Manager of the LNWR describes the works on p108-118.

1890
Engineer, Vol 70 (1890), p234.
Brief account of visit by the Society of Engineers.

1899
ISI, 1899, ii, p267-9.
Description of a visit to the Works by the Iron and Steel Institute.

1891
Locomotive Engineering, (Dec 1892, p449, 451, 453, 455).
'The Crewe shops of the LNW, the largest in Great Britain'
A well illustrated article explaining English methods to American engineers. Valuable for its detail.

1892-3
English Illustrated Magazine, (1892-3, p377-91).
Cooke, C. J. Bowen, 'LNW Locomotive Works at Crewe'
Description of the works by the then Assistant Running Superintendent, Locomotive Department.

1893
Edward Arnold,
Round the Works of our Great Railways, [1893].
A well illustrated description is given by C. J. Bowen Cooke on p1-34.

1894
IMechE, 1894, p458-61.
Plates 106 and 107 are useful plans of the works.
Brief description of a visit by the IMechE.

1895
LNWR. Visit of the International Congress of Railway Engineers to Crewe Works.
Description of the LNWR company's locomotive works at Crewe. LNWR, June, 1895.
A useful pamphlet which contains a plan of the works.

1896
Engineer, Vol 82 (1896), p 39.
Description of a visit by the Manchester Association of Engineers.

1897
Canadian Engineer, (May, June, 1897).
'British Railway Enterprise' (the LNWR).
The May article has little of interest but the June article is a well illustrated account of the works.

1898
Cassier's Magazine, Vol 12 (1897), p687-94.
'Electric power in a Great Railway Shop: an interview with F. W. Webb ...'
A valuable article, well illustrated with photographs, including an electrically driven drilling machine and Webb's electric tube-cutter.

1897-1902
Railway Magazine, Vol 54 (1924), p271-6, 382-6; Correspondence, p406-7.
Sams, J. C. B., 'Recollections of Crewe, 1897-1902'
Valuable picture of working conditions and methods at Crewe, during a period of transition from the old system to 'assembly line' methods.

1903
Cassier's Magazine, Vol 24 (1903), p393-407, 519-33.
Lake, Charles S., 'The Railway Town of Crewe'
A detailed and well illustrated history and description of the works.

2e Crewe and Webb's Civic Activities

'You know very well that I sit here as an independent Mayor,
and will not allow, if I can help it, any politics to interfere
with me, and I think it has been shown that I, myself, have
never interfered in the politics of this town ...'

F. W. Webb

(*Crewe Guardian*, 26th February, 1887, p5)

In a town which is virtually the creation of a single company, it is inevitable that at some stage town and company will come into conflict, that there will be rebellion against the paternalism of the company.

At Crewe this conflict took a particularly bitter form. Led by Councillor Hodgson, a Crewe doctor who later became Sir William, the local Liberals protested against LNWR participation in local government and accused Webb and his fellow officials of supporting the Tories, although they called themselves 'Independents', and of victimising Liberal employees.

The trouble appears to have started in 1880 when a committee of foremen was set up to assist the company's 'Independent' nominees to the Town Council.[1] Ironically, in the first Borough election, in November 1877, it was the Tories who complained that the Works foremen were intimidating the men to vote for the 'Independent Railway Company Liberal' candidates.[2] The first major charges of intimidation were made in 1885 after about 150 men had been discharged. Many were Liberals; only one was a Tory. The latter appealed and was reinstated.[3] The Liberal *Crewe Chronicle* made accusations against Webb in the issue of 26th September 1885,[4] but this was only the beginning of the 'Intimidation Affair'.

There was more trouble during the election of a new alderman in February 1887, when Councillor Hodgson submitted a resolution: 'that we enter an emphatic protest against the method adopted by the officials of the Railway Company who have seats on the Town Council of filling the vacancies which occur among the aldermen from time to time by the appointment of Tories to the seats vacated by Liberals, the palpable effect of which is the creation of a local governing body out of harmony with the sympathies of the people and the discouragement of free political organisation among the residents of the borough.'[5]

Further accusations were made at a meeting of the Park Committee in August 1889, when there was a heated discussion over a keep-off-the-grass bye-law. Councillor Hodgson said that it seemed to him that it was 'becoming popular with the highest authorities' of that town to 'institute an elaborate system of espionage, accompanied by penalties, for small offences'; and continued with an accusation of political discrimination: 'If this bye-law was passed and the unfortunate individual who was brought before the magistrates and fined happed to be a Radical, he would be dismissed from his work in the railway works.'[1]

The Liberals were not going to miss any opportunity to make their grievances known. In November 1889 the matter was brought to a head. At the election meeting of the new mayor, Councillor Hodgson openly accused the Independent Railway Company representatives of acting exclusively in the Tory interest and asked for an explanation of their conduct. The atmosphere of the meeting can be gauged from the open hostility shown to Webb: 'I have no doubt that when you, Mr Chairman [Webb], get up you will give us some defence. (Ironical laughter). You are the only man who is in a position to give an adequate defence, because from the position you hold your opinion must always be held in the greatest respect and veneration among us. (Laughter and applause).'[2]

Webb offered no 'defence' and at the Town Council meeting of 27th November Councillor Hodgson pressed the point further by moving that a memorial be sent to the next meeting of the LNWR shareholders. It started: 'Your memorialists desire to call your attention to the fact that the chief officials ... at Crewe have for some years been using their official influence as managers ... to create the impression in the minds of the railway company's employees that their association with Liberal organisations will jeopardize their prospects of promotion, and even of their permanent employment under the company ... For nine long years the managers of the works and their subordinate foremen have been allied with the Tories of Crewe to crush Liberalism altogether out of the town.'[3]

Two specific accusations were then made: first, that the Company's representatives had never supported a Liberal for membership to the Town Council but had, under the guise of being Independents, always supported Tory candidates; second, 'By intimidation and persecution of your Liberal workmen, and by making the chance of promotion depend upon subserviency to the Tory political demands of the management, they have created a state of political serfdom in the works which is simply intolerable to some of your best and

(1) Chaloner, p153-5.
(2) *ibid*, p147.
(3) *ibid*, p156-7. Interesting 'side-effects' of this matter are given in an article by Neil Fraser in *RCHS*, Vol 9 (1963), p49-51.
(4) *ibid*, p308.
(5) *CG*, 26th February 1887, p5.

(1) *CG*, 31st August 1889, p5.
(2) *CC*, 16th November 1889, p2: also reported *CG* 13th November 1889, p3.
(3) *CG*, 30th November 1889, p4-5; also reported *CC*, 30th November 1889, and *Times*, 28th November 1889, p10.

most faithful servants now in your employ.'

The memorial concluded: 'Your memorialists therefore pray that your directors may be instructed to declare once for all that the men in Crewe works shall not be interfered with in the exercise of their political rights.'

Councillor Hodgson said that the trouble began in the period 1879-1880 when, shortly after a Liberal victory in the council elections, the company officials started local government activity as 'Independents'. ('The only thing the Independents had shown their independence in was that they were independent of Liberal politics'). Then had followed interference in the personal political views of the men in the Railway Works: 'It was the commonest thing in the world for the foremen and their understrappers to single out prominent Liberal workers and advise them in their own interest to discontinue their association with politics. The curious thing was that Tories were never singled out for the same advice ... Those frequent warnings spread a gloom over the town from 1880 to 1885, which he would never forget, and a state of terror existed in the town.'

The Town Council, with its Tory majority, voted against the sending of the memorial, but it had done its work. The papers were full of stories of intimidation, of accusations and counter accusations: the *Crewe Guardian* ('Neutral in all matters political and religious') was almost as sympathetic with the Hodgson campaign as was the Liberal *Crewe Chronicle*. Even the Grand Old Man himself sent a letter to the *Chronicle*, a letter so carefully composed that it was at once outraged and guarded.[1]

There were public meetings: one, held at the Town Hall on 2nd January 1890 'for the purpose of protesting against the unjust and untrue accusations', being broken up by men from the rival meeting held that evening in the Corn Exchange.[2] The *Crewe Chronicle* commented with its characteristic crude and caustic style of the period: '300 Tories met to deny the truth of the charge of persecution; 1200 Liberals (and perhaps a few honest Tories among them, who knows!) assemble and affirm and re-affirm the truth of the charges.'[3]

It is interesting to note that at the conclusion of the postponed Town Hall meeting, held on the 16th January, at least one Liberal (David Nield) spoke in support of the Company.[4]

The half yearly meeting of the LNWR Directors and Shareholders held on 20th February was a stormy affair. A group of Liberal shareholders, including Dr Hodgson who had bought £100 of stock the month before, raised the matter of intimidation and demanded an inquiry. On this occasion even the awesome Sir Richard Moon had some difficulty in convincing the meeting that there had been no intimidation and that an inquiry was unnecessary.[1]

The Times, as would be expected, was in sympathy with the LNWR. A company meeting had been used for political ends: 'Several of Mr Tomlinson's [ie Mr James Tomlinson's] fellow-speakers were shown yesterday to be newcomers into the Company's ranks, having recently bought small lots of shares by way of qualification; and we may thus suppose that their interest in politics and political self-advertisement is greater than their interest in the Company. Their evidence thus can hardly be said to carry much independent weight.'[2]

The leader writer suggests that as the dismissed men were 'not only Liberals but active politicians, given to platform appearances and public-house caucuses, they may have been found less useful in the yards than the Company had a right to expect'. He suggests too that they used their dismissals to full political advantage. 'Here, we imagine, is the explanation of the whole matter'.

While allowing that the returning of a Liberal member to Parliament and two Liberals out of three to the County Council seems proof that Crewe citizens had political freedom, *The Times* regrets that an inquiry was not set up: 'A Board of Directors, men of ability and sense, including politicians of all shades, are most unlikely to encourage, much less to order, a course of procedure which would infallibly make them exceedingly unpopular, not only throughout the country, but especially in their own capital city – for so Crewe may be fairly described'.

The Liberals had, apparently, been unsuccessful. They did not get the inquiry that they sought and there had been no admission of guilt by anyone associated with the company. At a Liberal meeting held in the Town Hall on the 26th March 1890, however, Mr McLaren was able to report a different atmosphere in the works: 'Mr McLaren thinks that the officials have received strong private hints that the directors will not tolerate any interference with the workmen such as that suggested, and this is more than probable, for since the meeting of share-holders things inside the works have been vastly different ... Since the exposure at the board-room in London, Crewe Works is described as a changed place. Mr McLaren does not think there will be any more intimidation of Liberals ...'[3]

In August, 1890, Webb resigned from his position as Alderman, and the next month Whale followed his example.[4] Wilmot Eardley, the Tory printer, saw their withdrawal from the Council as a misfortune 'almost equivalent to the loss of Counsel in a law suit, and it is to be feared that it will result in restricted privileges to the town through the want of direct advocacy to the Chairman and Directors ...'[5] The Council elected in

(1) *CC*, 21st December 1889, p8; also *Times*, 20th December 1889, p7, and full text given in Chaloner, p309-10.
(2) *CG*, 4th January 1890, p4; also reported *Times*, 4th January 1890, p3.
(3) *CC*, 11th January 1890, p8.
(4) *Times*, 17th January 1890, p5.

(1) *CG*, 22nd February 1890, p5; *CC*, 22nd February 1890, p5, 8 and *Times*, 21st February 1890, p9, 12.
(2) *Times*, 21st February 1890, p9.
(3) *CC*, 29th March, 1890, p8.
(4) *CG*, 30th August 1890, and *CC* 30th August, 1890, p5, 8.
(5) *Eardley's Almanack*, 1891, p4.

November 1891 consisted of twenty Liberals and four Tories.[1]

A number of questions arise out of the Intimidation Affair. Was it indeed anything more than a figment of the Liberal mind, a case of over-sensitivity in a town created by a private company? There can be no doubt that some Liberals were forced out of the Works by the hostility of the foremen: Joseph Jones, Chairman of the Crewe Liberal Association, and William Urquhart, Secretary of the Crewe Liberal Club, were the oft-quoted examples. Both had given long service to the Company, Jones twenty three years and Urquhart thirty three. Urquhart may have been something of a trouble-maker for he had taken an active part in the demonstrations opposing the compulsory pension fund held at the beginning of 1889, and he was a strong union man. If there was systematic victimisation of the Liberals, however, what was the reason behind it, and who was responsible for it?

Webb's character precludes the possibility of his having personal political ambitions. Even the *Crewe Chronicle*, his bitter opponent, had to admit that: 'It was his one weakness, perhaps, that he detested speech-making, and never overcame his distaste to public appearances.' [2]

When he was approached to offer himself as Mayor, in 1886, the *Chronicle* did not think that he would accept the offer [3] and indeed Webb expressed his disinclination in his election speech: 'This honour is not one of my own seeking. Having been requested by representatives of the most influential body of the citizens of this town, I have felt it my duty to waive all private objections and enter the arena ...' [4]

These are not the qualities or attitude of a man thirsting for political power and his bitterest opponents never suggested that he sought it. Suspicion now turns on the Company: had there been a directive from Euston to get into the town's government and ensure Tory supremacy? It was a pro-Company correspondent to *The Times* who pointed out that the LNWR paid one-third of the town's rates, unaware that he was giving a possible motive for Company involvement in Crewe local government:[5] control of the Council would ensure that the rates were kept down.

In fact, however, the Liberals never suggested that Euston had any hand in the matter, and stressed that they had no quarrel with the Directors but only with the Company's officials at Crewe. They considered that Dr James Atkinson was the man behind all the trouble. Atkinson was the Company's surgeon, the first Mayor of Crewe, and leader of the Crewe Conservative Party. He was also a personal friend of Webb. It was Atkinson whom the Liberals saw as the man who influenced Webb politically.

'Councillor Atkinson was the first to interfere [said Hodgson] ... They [the Liberals] knew full well that he had been at the bottom of the interference. They believed that Alderman Webb's generous feelings, which he could manifest when left alone, would not have allowed that interference if he had not been influenced in a wrong direction.' [1]

Councillor Charles Welch, during the Memorial debate, also made the same point, but without mentioning names: 'If Mr Webb was left alone he was a gentleman, but he was so susceptible to influences that had been brought to bear upon him that he did things which he must afterwards regret.' [2]

And Councillor Hodgson did likewise on the retirement of Webb from the Town Council: 'He always felt that Mr Webb was not the greatest sinner. If he had been left to the generous impulses of his own, they would not have had so many passages of arms.' [3]

The full story of this unfortunate episode will probably never be revealed but it shows an interesting side of Webb's character. His failure in local government seems to arise out of political naiveté. He thought it possible to exclude party considerations from local affairs and frequently appealed for united effort in town business: 'I have said on previous occasions, and I am not ashamed to say it again, that I hope we shall not have a divided Crewe, for as surely as we have, so surely will our Barque be sunk.' [4] (This Crew(e) pun became something of a chestnut and was ridiculed by the Liberals as 'Mr Webb's only pun').

'Let us not raise questions as to who proposes and who seconds this or that, but ask always, "Is it good for the town?" and let us give an independent answer, and go on and prosper.' [5] Associated with this idealistic approach was his belief that he was himself free of party politics: 'He [Webb] found himself that there was so much dishonesty in politics – he did not care whether on one side or the other – that he kept entirely away from them.' [6]

He did not seem to appreciate that, although he did not belong or give conscious support to any party, he was by upbringing, position, and indeed by temperament, a Tory, that his 'natural' attitude was Tory.

Although Webb's involvement in civic affairs may appear regrettable, there were brighter aspects and Crewe benefited on many occasions from his generosity. His two terms of office as Mayor were comparatively happy and trouble-free. The 'Intimidation' incidents during this period were mild.

Webb was elected Mayor in Jubilee year, 1887 – the Jubilee year of both the Queen and of Crewe – in the hope that he might receive one of the honours that the Queen would be bestowing on local dignitaries.

(1) Chaloner, p166.
(2) *CC*, 9th June 1906, p5.
(3) *CC*, 6th November 1886, p8: 'Failing his acceptance of the position – it is understood that he does not care for it ...'
(4) *CC*, 13th November 1886, p5.
(5) *Times*, 4th January 1890, p3.

(1) *CG*, 13th November 1889, p3.
(2) *CG*, 30th November 1889, p4-5; quoted Chaloner, p153 (second footnote).
(3) *CG*, 30th August 1890, p4.
(4) *CC*, 6th November 1886, p8.
(5) *CG*, 21st July 1888, p4.
(6) *CG*, 18th November 1890, p3.

Alderman McNeill, in a flight of fancy, even spoke of Sir Francis William Webb and Lady Webb.[1] The 'working men of Crewe' opened a subscription, maximum contribution of one penny per man, and bought his aldermanic robes.[2] Unfortunately, neither honour nor lady came to Mr Webb.

He was re-elected the following year (1888), specifically to enable him to be Mayor in the year that Queen's Park was opened. Webb had negotiated with the LNWR with the result that the Company had given the land for the park and donated £10,000 for laying it out. (The story that the site had been chosen to block the approach of the Great Western Railway does not appear to have any foundation.[3])

After the 'Intimidation' trouble of 1889-1890 was forgotten there were exchanges of good-will between Webb and the town he had helped to create. In June 1900, when the 4000th engine emerged from the Works, he was given the freedom of the town, and the following year he presented a loving-cup to the town in recognition of his fifty years association with Crewe.[4]

Webb was largely responsible for the formation of the Crewe Volunteer Engineer Corps which sent 400 skilled railway men to serve with the Royal Engineers in the South African War. Various medical institutions in Crewe owed their existence to Webb. Crewe Memorial Cottage Hospital, which was officially opened on 7th August 1895, was the result of generosity by the LNWR, which provided the land, and Webb and a director of the Lancashire & Yorkshire Railways, Henry Yates Thompson, each of whom donated £1,000. The profits from the Euston Coffee Tavern, established by Webb in 1880, latterly went to the Memorial Cottage Hospital, and shortly before his death Webb gave a further cheque for £5,000 towards the upkeep of the hospital.

Two institutions were founded with money bequeathed by Webb. He left £10,000 for a nursing service for 'persons of the poorer classes ... in the bor-

ough of Crewe',[1] which established the Webb Nursing Institute, and the residue of his estate, £50,000, was left to found an orphanage for the children of employees of the LNWR.[2] The Webb Orphanage was opened on the 18th December 1911, and has only recently outlived its task. It is now to be a hostel for young men attending the Crewe Locomotive Works Training School.

Thus it will be seen that, although Webb could be heavy-handed in his relations with the town - as when he wrote in 1877: ' ... if the people of Crewe do not study the Company's interest, I shall not be responsible for what the directors will do in reference to putting on the rates.' [3] - he had a genuine concern for the prosperity of the town and the welfare of his employees.

Upon his death the *Crewe Guardian* suggested that a suitable memorial to Webb might take the form of a bronze statue in Queen's Park.[4] The idea was taken up with some enthusiasm, a particularly keen correspondent signing himself 'ONE WHO LOVED AND ADMIRED HIM'.[5] Unfortunately, the idea was not so well received by the officials of the LNWR and the matter came to nothing.[6] One wonders how far the animosity of Webb's successor, George Whale, accounts for the attitude of the Company.

In a speech to the annual meeting of the Crewe Mechanics' Institution in February 1887, Webb had said, with reference to Sir Joseph Whitworth: 'It was very often the case – too often, indeed – that their greatest friends and benefactors were very soon forgotten. They only had to look around them and mark the many benefactors who had lived in their own town even, and to note how very very seldom they were spoken about'.[7]

(1) CC, 13th November 1886 p5.
(2) CC, 4th December 1886, p8.
(3) Chaloner, foot-note, p90.
(4) NUR. *Official souvenir of the annual meeting of delegates ... 1923, at ... Crewe*, p58.

(1) Chaloner, p182.
(2) *Railway Magazine*, Vol 29 (1911),p 485-6; *Railway and Travel Monthly*, Vol 3 (1911), p492.
(3) Chaloner, p 146. (1) CG, 9th June, 1906, p4.
(4) CG, 9th June 1906, p4.
(5) CG, 13th June 1906, p4.
(6) CG, 30th June 1906, p4.
(7) CG, 26th February 1887, p4.

A note on sources.

As is evident from the foregoing foot-note references, the main sources for this aspect of Webb's activities are Dr W. H. Chaloner's *Social and Economic Development of Crewe* (1950) and the local newspapers.

Dr Chaloner provides a thorough study of the Intimidation Affair but it is necessary to re-examine it specifically in terms of Webb's position and character. It is also necessary, as the Rev J. S. Cowen found [1], to supplement his tendency to Liberal, non-conformist bias. There was a Company view of the matter, expressed in *The Times*, for example, but this is not given in Dr Chaloner's work.

The Liberal view was also given in the *Crewe Chronicle*, a paper cruder in every way than its fellow the *Crewe Guardian*. It gave less space to Crewe Town news but made up for this by the virulence of its attacks upon the Tory faction and upon Mr Webb.

There are long files of both of these papers at the British Museum Newspaper Library, Colindale, but due to bombing neither file is complete. For some years, 1898 for example, copies of both papers have been destroyed. Holdings in Crewe and district are slight. The Public Library has the *Guardian* from 1912 and the *Chronicle* from 1956. The Nantwich office of the *Guardian* has an incomplete file from 1892. The Chester office of the *Chronicle* has a file covering 1874 to 1915 and 1920 to date: the Crewe office holds a file from 1931 to date, excluding 1945.[2] The later volumes of the papers are not to be overlooked. The *Guardian*, for example, published long and useful biographical articles whenever the opportunity arose. There was one in May 1934, in the series 'Men who made Crewe' [3] and another in 1936, the centenary of Webb's birth.[4] These articles frequently repeated anecdotes and quoted speeches which would be difficult to trace in the earlier volumes of the paper.

(1) J. S. Cowen, *Church and People in a Cheshire Town* [ie Crewe]. Thesis in part requirement for the final year Post-Ordination Studies in the Diocese of Chester, 1962.
(2) Information supplied by the Editor.
(3) *CG*, 4th May 1934, p7.
(4) *CG*, 22nd May 1936, p8-9.

Other Material

Portraits

In his *Dictionary of National Biography* article, William Forbes Spear notes the existence of two portraits in oils and two busts of Webb. One portrait, by Charles H. Charnock, a blacksmith at Crewe Works, is a poor thing which after many years in the board-room of the Memorial Cottage Hospital has now found its rightful place in the cellar there.[1] The G. Hall Neale portrait is a fine piece of work and still hangs in the board-room at the Orphanage. This is an undated version but it was presented to the Orphanage in April 1912. There is another version, this one dated 1903, which is now in the British Transport Museum at Clapham.

Replicas of the bust by Sir Henry B. Robinson of Corwen, are still to be seen at the Orphanage and at the Memorial Cottage Hospital. The story of this bust was often told in the *Crewe Guardian*: 'When Mr Webb was on a visit to him, Sir Henry's children were playing with some wet clay. Mr Webb began to play with them. At length Sir Henry suggested that he should make a model of Mr Webb. The latter agreed, and the work occupied about five years. Mr Webb would not sit for more than five minutes at a time and had a habit of going to sleep. At length, Sir Henry warned him that if he went to sleep again, he (Sir Henry) would go out for a walk. Suddenly Mr Webb appeared to be sleeping, Sir Henry left the room, and on returning he found that instead of going to sleep, Mr Webb had been busy on the bust. He had modelled two horns, one on each side of the head, had turned up the moustache, and pulled down the beard – the result being a remarkable likeness to Mephistopheles!'[2]

This story provides a rare glimpse of the private life of Webb, and of a personality which was usually hidden behind the Railway Official. It is unfortunate that the bust itself provides no such insight but merely records the hard exterior of the man.

Apart from these portraits and busts noted by Spear, there is also a half relief head of Webb on the drinking fountain in Queen's Park, Crewe.

(1) The information on the present whereabouts of the portraits and busts in Crewe was provided by Mr C. Nulty who also supplied me with photographs.
(2) *CG*, 22nd May, 1936, p8: the story is also told in the same newspaper for 22nd May 1927 and 4th May 1934.

Photographs

Many of the photographs in the negative collection at Crewe Works, to which reference is made in section 3e, consist of groups of visitors accompanied by Webb, frequently in the porch of No. 1 Chester Place (the 'official residence' of the CME at Crewe). These include:
(a) Group with Ramsbottom taken in 1885. (BR LM Region neg DM 9007).
(b) Webb with the directors of the Great North of Scotland Railway, taken in 1892. (BR LM Region neg DM 9011)

(c) Photograph of the G. Hall Neale portrait. (BR LM Region neg DM 9014).
(d) Group outside No. 1 Chester Place which includes Webb and R. F. Roberts. (Crewe neg A37).
(e) Group including Trevithick and Ramsbottom, reproduced in O. S. Nock's *The LNWR* (p 37). (Crewe neg A38).
(f) Webb with a group outside the General Offices. He is wearing a grey topper. (Crewe neg A69).
(g) Group including Webb. (Crewe neg A2).
(h) Webb with the directors of the Caledonian Railway, taken in 1885. (Crewe neg A52).
(i) Webb in the mayoral chain of office. (BR LM Region Derby neg E53).

The following reproductions of photographs have been traced:

In books
W. H. Chaloner, *The Social and Economic Development of Crewe*. Facing p160.
C. Hamilton Ellis, *Twenty Locomotive Men*. Webb holding a photograph of *Greater Britain*. Facing p140.
O. S. Nock, *The London and North Western Railway*. Facing p37 and 91.
O. S. Nock, *The Premier Line*. Facing p39
O. S. Nock, *The Railway Race to the North*. Facing p33.
O. S. Nock, *Steam Locomotive*. Facing p96.

In Periodicals
Cassier's Magazine, Vol 10 (1896), p82.
Cassier's Magazine, Vol 24 (1903), p470. Webb holding a photograph of *Greater Britain*. This same photograph also appears in Ellis's *Twenty Locomotive Men*.
Eardley's Crewe Almanack, 1888, p6.
Engineer, Vol 101 (1906), p579.
Engineering, Vol 81 (1906), p764.
LRCWR, Vol 45 (1939), p179.
Railroad Gazette, Vol 35 (1903), p423.
Railway Magazine, Vol 5 (1889), p232. Webb in his mayoral robes and chain of office.
Railway Magazine, Vol 6 (1900), p98.
Railway Magazine, Vol. 88 (1942), p159.
Railway Magazine, Vol 107 (1961), p756.
Railway Magazine, Vol.107 (1961), p841. The same group photograph as used in Mr Nock's *The LNWR*, p37.

Preserved engines

Two Webb engines have been preserved. *Hardwicke*, after spending many years in the Paint Shop at Crewe Works, can now be seen at the British Transport Museum at Clapham, and the last Webb engine in service, the 0-6-2 Coal Tank engine originally numbered 1054 (becoming LMS No. 7799 and finally British Railways No. 58926) has been saved by a preservation fund organised by Mr J. M. Dunn.[1] At the time of writing (July 1963) the tank engine is to be seen

(1) *SLS*, Vol 37 (1961), p230-2: J. M. Dunn, 'I Buy a Locomotive'.

at the Railway Preservation Society's depot at Hednesford, Staffordshire, but it is shortly to be moved to Caernarvonshire where it will be permanently exhibited in the National Trust's Industrial Locomotive Museum, at Penrhyn Castle, Bangor.

Models

For some reason Webb engines are not very popular with model makers. Occasionally, and only occasionally, one sees such a model: there is, for example, an 'O' scale model of the four-cylinder compound *Black Diamond* (No. 1905) by Bernard Miller, illustrated in the *Model Railway News*, Vol 40 (1963), p88-9.

Two model kits are available commercially but both make the same engine. N. and K.C. Keyser Ltd (of 101 Tubbs Road, Willesden, London, NW10) manufacture a kit for constructing a metal '00' scale model of the 0-6-2 Coal Tank engine. Douglass Models (of Broad Carr Lane, Holywell Green, Halifax) produce a kit for making a bondaglass 'O' scale model of the same locomotive.

Various models are mentioned in C. Hamilton Ellis's *Model Railways, 1838-1939*, most of which bear little resemblance to Crewe products except that they have LNWR livery.

Such small scale models do little except illustrate the popularity, or otherwise, of particular engines. The large scale models that are to be found in museums have greater usefulness. They can be used to demonstrate the action of the valve gear and the motion and can thus show kinematically various points that the photograph and the drawing are unable to display.

Three such large scale models have been traced:
(a) *King Edward VII* (No. 1942). This gilded bronze model of an 'Alfred the Great' 4-4-0 locomotive stands in a case on the South African War Memorial in Queen's Park, Crewe. The half-section pattern for this model – 'executed by Robert Bebbington' – can be seen in the entrance hall of the Railway Veterans Institute.
(b) *Jubilee* (No. 1901) can be seen at the Transport Museum, Clapham and is, presumably, the model appearing in a series of the Crewe Works photographs. [1]
(c) *Marchioness of Stafford* (No. 2798). This model of a 'Dreadnought' class compound is to be seen at the Science Museum, South Kensington.

There is evidence of the existence of at least two further models. There are photographs of a model of *Dreadnought* (No. 503) among the Crewe Works collection,[2] and there is reference made in Mr Sams's *Railway Magazine* article to a half-inch-to-the-foot scale model of the 'Teutonic' class engine *Jeanie Deans* (No. 1304). [3]

I have been unable to trace the present location of these models.

(1) Crewe negatives A407, A408 and A409.
(2) Crewe negatives A410 and A411.
(3) *Railway Magazine*, Vol 54 (1924), p385.

Drawings

A primary source of the greatest value has survived in the Drawing Office at Crewe Works. This is a collection of most, if not all, of the general arrangement and detail drawings of the Webb locomotives. It is difficult to describe and assess such a large collection but the following selection will give some idea of the nature of these drawings and their value in ascertaining, confirming and illustrating technical details.

(1) '4ft 3in Six wheels Coupled Coal Engine'.
Dated September 1872 (C29128)*.
Side elevation, sectional plan and four half end elevations to the scale 1½ inches to 1 foot.
This drawing for the '17 inch Coal Engine' bears some interesting alterations. The Ramsbottom form of horizontally hinged smoke-box door has been replaced by a vertically hinged door, the inclined front of the smoke-box has been made perpendicular, and the braking arrangement has been modified.
(2) 'Webb's 3 cylinder Compound Passenger Engine': [*Dreadnought*]. (C35006)*.
Dated August 1884.
Side elevation and seven half end elevations to the scale 1½ inches to 1 foot.
This drawing shows, among other things, the arrangement of the three cylinders.
(3) '7ft Compound Passenger Engine: eight wheeler': [*Greater Britain*]. (C29125)*. Dated October 1891.
Sectional side elevation and sectional plan to the scale 1½ inches to 1 foot.
This shows the combustion chamber and ash-hopper in the long boiler.
Drawing C29124 consists of six half end elevations of this engine.
(4) '7ft 0in Four wheels Coupled Passenger Engine'. (C32544)*. Dated June 1897.
Side elevation and sectional plan to the scale 1½ inches to 1 foot.
This is the experimental form of *Jubilee* (No. 1501) with four cylinders (all 15in by 24in) simple, and a double chimney. It not only shows the lay-out of the four cylinders in line and of the double chimney, but also illustrates the use of the radial truck, and the employment of piston valves.
(5) '7ft 0in four wheels Coupled Compound Passenger Engine. General arrangement of radial truck'. (13283)*. Dated December 1899.
Side elevation, plan and two half end elevations to the scale 3 inches to 1 foot.
This, presumably, is the radial truck for the 'Jubilee' class engines which were built in 1899 and 1900.

* Crewe Drawing Office reference number.

Photographs

An attempt was made to index all illustrations of Webb locomotives but this was soon found to be a colossal and unrewarding labour. Good photographs of most of the engines are quite common, but 'static' pictures (with the engine standing in the Works or at a station) are far more numerous than 'action' photographs. Admittedly the static picture is more useful for checking technical details but the photographs of engines in steam and at work are more interesting and impressive. These are so uncommon that it is worth drawing attention to some specific examples:

Railway World, Vol 16 (1955), p29. Photograph by R. J. Purves of a 'Jumbo' and train on Shap

Railway World, Vol 22 (1961), p186. 'Jubilee' class engine *Irresistible* hauling a train out of Euston.

Trains Illustrated, No. 1 (1946), p18. A train hauled by two compounds, a 'Dreadnought' and a 'Teutonic'.

Trains Illustrated, Vol 8 (1955), p112. Photograph by F. R. Hebron of an 0-6-2 Coal Tank (LMS No.7720) and its train leaving the Britannia Tubular Bridge.

Other good 'action' photographs are to be found in C. Hamilton Ellis's *British Trains of Yesteryear* and those of H. Gordon Tidey should be particularly noted.

There are a number of collections of photographs which will furnish most of the illustrative material required for a study of the locomotives.[1] These are:

(a) Locomotive Publishing Company Ltd.,
Craven House, Hampton Court, Surrey.

This consists of the F. Moore and Bleasdale collections. A catalogue, covering only part of the collection, has been issued.

(b) Real Photographs Company Ltd,
Victoria House, Southport, Lancashire.

This includes the Whitworth and H. Gordon Tidey collections. Lists are issued; Nos. R22, T1, W1, W3, W4, W5 and W8 cover Webb engines.

(c) Crewe Works

There is a large collection of valuable photographs of locomotives, groups of people (many including Webb), and of Webb's inventions.

Requests for prints should be made to the Public Relations and Publicity Officer, London Midland Region, British Railways, Euston House, London. NW1. There is a three volume manuscript index to this collection to be seen at Crewe.

(d) Science Museum.

A portfolio of large, mounted photographs, three of which (*Compound*, *Greater Britain* and a photograph of the drawings for a three-cylinder compound engine) are signed by Webb.

(e) There is a reference in the *Railway Magazine* [2] to a collection of photographs which Webb presented to Mr Charles S. Lake. I have been unable to trace the present location of this collection.

One of Webb's engines was the subject of an early film. *The Locomotive Magazine* in 1899 reproduced a still from a British Mutoscope & Biograph Company 'ribbon' showing *Jeanie Deans* taking water near Bushey while travelling at about 60mph.[3]

There is one film commercially available today which contains shots of Webb engines: *LNWR Locos in 1950* (Black and white, 16mm and 8mm, issued by Colourviews Ltd, Factory Road, Aston Fields, Bromsgrove, Worcester).

This film, made by the TV 'Railway Roundabout' team of John Adams and Patrick Whithouse, contains shots of an 0-6-2 radial tank engine, a 5ft 6in 2-4-2 tank on the Dudley Motor Train, a 'Cauliflower' on the Keswick line, 0-6-2 'Coal Tank' engines working in South Wales, and a '17in Coal Engine 0-6-0. There are also shots of *Hardwicke* and *Cornwall* in retirement at Crewe Works.

Sound Recordings

Unfortunately there are no recordings of the compound engines but their sound has been described by two writers. Mr Nock has described the 'Webb three-cylinder compounds, with their one low-pressure cylinder [which] had an acoustic quality that distinguished them among all others; they had only half the normal number of exhaust "puffs", and in the distance it sounded as if the train was approaching at about half its actual speed'. [1]

Mr E. B. Hall has also drawn attention to 'the extraordinary exhaust note of the three-cylinder compounds when the big low-pressure cylinder began to function. The beat of this dominated all other sounds, and I have frequently been able to decide quite definitely the type of engine on an approaching train, even at a distance of two miles or so – more on a still day. It was a most fascinating sound to me!' [2]

There is one recording containing the sounds of a Webb simple engine: Transacord record No. 5036-7 *The LNWR 0-8-0*. This record features Bowen Cooke's 0-8-0s but section one on the second side is a recording of the Stephenson Locomotive Society special last train run on the Abergavenny-Merthyr line on 5th January 1958. On this run the 0-8-0, No. 49121, was piloted by the ex-LNWR Webb 'Coal Tank' engine, BR No. 58926, which has since been acquired by a preservation society.

Mr Peter Handford, the director of Transacord Limited, reports that the above recording 'had to be taken out of production last year and is no longer available, but if all goes well, it is possible that we may re-issue extracts from this record as an EP in the new series of records which are now produced from our recordings by the Argo Record Company'.

Mr. Handford did not know of any other recordings of Webb engines: 'In view of the date at which they disappeared from service it seems most unlikely that there are any other recordings, even of an amateur nature, since it is only in recent years, with the advent of inexpensive light weight recorders, that amateur recordings have been possible on any scale.' [3]

The BBC sound recordings of locomotives have been made for 'effects' and cannot be identified as specific engines.[4]

(1) The obvious source for photographs, the Radio Times Hulton Picture Library, was unable to trace anything relevant.
(2) *Railway Magazine*, Vol 88 (1942) May-June. Caption to plate.
(3) *Locomotive Magazine*, Vol 4 (1899), p145.

(1) O. S. Nock. *British Steam Railways*, p185.
(2) *Railway Magazine*, Vol 54 (1924), p407.
(3) Letter to the author dated 25th October, 1962.
(4) Letter from the BBC to the author dated 24th October, 1963.

Chronology

1836
21st May. Born at Tixall Rectory, second son of the Rector.

1847
Made a pony cart which was the pride of the village.

1851
11th August. Sent to Crewe as a pupil of F. Trevithick. Stayed with Robert Sherwin who had a barber's shop at the corner of Mill Street.

1859
February. Appointed Chief Draughtsman at the age of 22.

1861
September. Appointed Works Manager, at the age of 25.

1866-1871
'When I was not wanted'. Manager of the Bolton Iron & Steel Company.

1871
Summer. Visited the United States of America on behalf of the LNWR.

1871
1st October. Appointed Locomotive Superintendent of the LNWR.

1880-1885
First incidents in the 'Intimidation Affair'.

1886
9th November. Elected Mayor of Crewe.

1887
November. Re-elected Mayor.

1889-1890
Crisis of the 'Intimidation Affair'.

1889
5th December. Mr Gladstone's letter.

1890
2nd January, 16th January. Crewe meetings.

10th February. LNWR Shareholders' meeting.

27th August
Retirement from the Town Council.

24th September. Mr Whale's retirement from the Town Council.

1895
August. Opening of Crewe Memorial Cottage Hospital.

1900
16th June
Freedom of the Town given on the occasion of the completion of the 4000th engine.

1901
12th August. Fifty years at Crewe. Loving cup presented to the Town in recognition.

1903
Retirement after break-down of health.

1906
4th June. Died at Bournemouth.

1911
18th December. Webb Orphanage opened.

Index

End of Bibliography

Notes, Comments and Queries 2011

Nothing stays the same, and in the almost fifty years since John Spink wrote his bibliography, many things have changed. Institutions no longer exist or have been altered in some way, and buildings which were built for one purpose now serve another, or have been demolished altogether. Museums have closed and new ones opened. Exhibits and artefacts are no longer in the same location. Even Crewe Works has been reduced in size and importance to a fraction of what it was both in Webb's day and in 1965.

The following notes, therefore, are intended to bring the information in the bibliography up to date in 2011, and also to explain references and phrases that were easily understood at the time of writing but which now are perhaps less so. Although this section endeavours to solve these problems, however, inevitably there is much that is still unknown. Many questions, therefore, are asked but remain unanswered.

Many people have helped by providing information which appears in the section which follows, and profound thanks are due to: Don Adnitt, Sue Chambers, Brian Harris, Harry Jack, Norman Lee, Peter Ollerhead, Martin O'Keefe, David Patrick, Graham Roberts and John Wardle.

Anyone who can add anything to the information in this book is invited to contact the London & North Western Railway Society. All correspondence will be gratefully received.

1a – The Importance of F. W. Webb

Page 1: On his death, Prof W. H. Chaloner's material was sold to Waseda University, Tokyo, Japan, and is believed to be available for research in the university's library.

Page 3: Sellar and Yeatman were the authors of *1066 and all that* - so a 'broad brush' approach, which sets out to be witty about historical events and not necessarily to record them accurately.

Page 5: The 'Old Hospital' was situated in Liverpool Terrace, hence the reference to vibration from trains on the Liverpool line. There was another hospital, which was built by the LNWR for its employees, and catered for those injured in accidents in Crewe Works. It was at the end of Mill Street and occupied part of the Old Works.

Page 5: Are the scholarships at Liverpool and Manchester Universities still operating?

Page 5: The Institution of Civil Engineers Webb Prize was instituted in 1908, following a bequest by Francis William Webb, a former Vice-President of the Institution. Two prizes, each comprising a premium of £65 and a certificate, are awarded annually for papers on railway engineering and transportation in general.

There was a Webb Bequest to the Institution of Civil Engineers made from the will dated 22 May 1903 for the provision of a prize to the author of a paper on railway machinery. It appears to have been amalgamated into the ICE in 1963 along with a number of other similar bequests.

Also from the Charity Commissioners website is the Webb Relief in Sickness Fund, also known as the Webb Crewe Works Charity Fund, which continues to make grants to people in the Crewe area. The Webb Orphans' Fund was removed as a charity in 2003 and the funds transferred; presumably, this has some connection.

Page 5: Mr Slight was presumably in charge of the photographic department.

Page 5: The 'new type of big express goods engines' refers to the '18in Goods 0-6-0' commonly known as 'Cauliflowers'.

1b – Narrative of the Search and Compilation

Page 7: The whereabouts of F. W. Webb's papers remains unknown.

Page 8: The model of *King Edward VII* is now displayed in the entrance hall of Crewe Municipal Offices. The black paint has been removed, and the brass metal beneath is now highly polished.

Page 8: Stanway Manor. Webb bought the 550 acre estate for £12,000 in 1889 (memorandum of agreement signed by Webb 23rd November 1889). Arthur G. Hill, of Market Street Crewe, acted for him. The house is described as 'a substantially erected mansion', the estate comprised 'three desirable farms, three cottages, woods, ponds, plantations etc'. It was originally offered for sale at a much higher figure and eventually withrawn from auction on 5th October 1888, so Webb bought at a very good price. The house together with some land was on the market in 1975(?) for £300,000. The details of the 'Model Farm' are contained in a brief article in *The Building News* for 18th December 1891. There is an excellent drawing of the newly erected farm buildings which Webb had a hand in designing. The narrow-gauge track seems to run behind the piggery (now posh accommodation) on the south-west side. It was used to transport feed from the food-mixing house to the various stock houses. The farm also had an 8hp steam engine to drive the food-mixing equipment and the threshing machine. This farm was at Upper Stanway to the north east of the manor and two fields away.

There is believed to be an article in *The Railway Magazine* but the exact reference has not yet been discovered.

Page 8: The Webb Orphanage is now disused but is kept in good condition while its owners find a new use for it.

Page 9: Where is the Paint Shop book now?

Page 9: Where is the large ledger of press cuttings about Crewe and the LNWR?

Page 9: The drawings and photographic negatives are now in the National Railway Museum.

Page 13: Crewe Cricket Club was disbanded a few years ago and joined forces with the Vagrants' Cricket Club, which no longer has the roller made by F. W. Webb. It is last known to have been in use at the Alexandra Athletic and Cricket ground in 1898, when FWW played the first ball on the new ground in a match against Nantwich, using the cricket bat he had made himself many years previously. The new ground, which was in the 'V' of the Liverpool and Manchester lines, was required because the old ground, just to the west of the station, was due to be swallowed up in the construction of the 'big dig', the construction of the tunnels carrying the goods lines to the north and to Manchester beneath the North Junction.

All trace of the roller and its subsequent history have been lost and after Webb's retirement, its importance as a relic may not have been recognised. Perhaps it was melted down for scrap during the war or perhaps it still survives unrecognised in the brambles behind some cricket pavilion in the Crewe area.

Page 14: Does any picture exist of the device on his personal letter heading?

Page 14: F. W Webb's health – see articles in LNWRS *Journal*.

Page 15: What happened to the '145 engineering books and engravings of the two Stephensons and of George Parker Bidder' he gave to the Mechanics' Institute?

Page 15: The London & North Western Railway Historical Society, formed in 1962, ceased to exist only a few years later, though the exact date is unknown. The London & North Western Railway Society was formed in 1973 and has about 700 members. It has a Study Centre housing its library and archives, and is the publisher of this book.

2b – F. W. Webb as inventor and member of the engineering institutions

Page 20: The four cast-iron eagles which 'still adorn Flag Lane bridge' are now located as follows: one is outside the Eagle Medical Centre, which is near where Eagle Bridge used to be; two are in the Heritage Centre; and one is at the Wistaston Road entrance to the Works.

Page 20: Richard Trevithick's stationary engine is now in the Science Museum, South Kensington.

Page 20: '...no one has satisfactorily shown where the Webb system [of compounding] failed.'
George Carpenter, authority on French compounds, friend of Chapelon and translator of Chapelon's *Le Locomotive a Vapeur*, states that the main defect was the incorrect ratio between the volumes of the high and low-pressure cylinders. The volume of the low-pressure cylinders should be three times that of the high-pressure cylinders, and the steam pipes and receiver linking the two should be proportioned in the same ratio.

Page 20: F. W. Webb resigned in 1885 and broke off all relations with the IMechE. A possible explanation is that his compounds were criticised by George Marié.

George Carpenter says that this explanation is entirely reasonable. André Marié was CME of the PLM and died in 1884. He had always been in favour of simple expansion rather than compounding, and so the Marié who criticised Webb, probably his son or brother, may well have adopted his views.

2c – The Locomotives

Page 34: The identity of 'Argus' is revealed in an article in *British Railway Journal*, Volume II, No. 17, page 344-5, as being an LNWR shareholder, William H. Moss.

Page 34: The withdrawal of the compounds, especially the three-cylinder compounds, and the conversion to simple of many of the others, in the period after Webb's retirement in May 1903 up to about 1910, is sometimes referred to as the 'massacre of the compounds'. Yet a large number of simple engine was also withdrawn at the same time, all the 'Problems', only renewed in the 1890s, many 'Jumbos' and many '17in Coal Engines'. The conclusion must be that the Whale administration decided that there were far too many small engines in service, both compound and simple.

Page 35: A neat external style – no note needed, only photos.

Page 35: 'Dolly Vardens'. Dolly Varden is a character in *Barnaby Rudge* by Dickens. She wore a type of hat which was later named after her. In a painting - 'Dolly Varden looking back at her lover' - it is an oval-shaped hat, worn down at the front.

S. S. Scott's MS notes (later printed in *Loco News & Railway Contractor* vol XI, 1922, p59) say that the first LNWR engine to have a cab was No 1102 (Rothwell L&C Goods) which was turned out from Crewe in early 1872 after rebuilding with a Crewe boiler and a narrow semi-circular cab, somewhat like some of the early GNR cabs. This cab was called by the men a 'Dolly Varden' (after a current popular song) but a cab of the new standard pattern was substituted about 1874.

The cover of the 'Dolly Varden Quadrille and some words of a 'novelty song' - dated 1872 - show hats which are down at the front and up at the back with both edges curving down - so maybe a bit like a GNR cab.

Page 36: 'Montague suggests that standardisation came with Whale.' Montague is mistaken. Joseph Locke, engineer of the Grand Junction Railway, told the board in December 1839, before Crewe Works or the LNWR had come into existence, that the time had come to design 'a new and improved type of engine of which as many parts as possible should be to one standard.' (*Locomotives in Profile Volume 2, 'The Crewe Type'*, Stuart, D. H. and Reed, Brian, Profile Publications, page 53).

This principle of standardisation was followed by all locomotive superintendents at Crewe. Trevithick built 2-2-2 passenger and 2-4-0 goods versions of the same design. When Ramsbottom succeeded him he too built only highly standardised designs and when he retired in 1871, forty per cent of the whole locomotive stock consisted of one class, the 'DX' 0-6-0, which had many parts, including the boiler, in common with his other classes, such as the 'Special Tank', 'Newton' 2-4-0 and

'Problem' 2-2-2, so that sixty per cent had the same boiler.

Though Webb's engines looked different (with cabs, redesigned chimneys and black paint), they were standard with Ramsbottom's and he continued the policy of standardisation, so that by the late 1890s the LNWR achieved a higher degree of locomotive standardisation than any other British railway before or since.

Whale introduced larger boilers and larger engines, which were necessary, but since they increased the number of components, actually reduced the overall degree of standardisation.

2e – Crewe and Webb's Civic Activities

Page 50: Crewe Memorial Hospital was located opposite the Orphanage and is now demolished. It was so called because its wards were named after benefactors in their memory. The three original wards were Heath Ward, Thompson Ward and Webb Ward. Heath Ward was paid for by the Martin Heath trustees and named after Martin Heath; Thompson Ward was named after Samuel Thompson, a director of the LNWR, whose nephew, Henry Yates Thompson donated £1000 (Henry had never, incidentally, visited Crewe); and Webb Ward was named after F. W. Webb, who also donated £1000. Other wards were added later and were also named after benefactors.

Before this hospital was opened, there was no hospital in Crewe other than an isolation hospital, and anyone in Crewe needing a hospital had to go to Nantwich.

The Webb Nursing Institute was located at No. 8 Heathfield Avenue (off Hightown, Crewe) and seems to have been what would now be termed a 'care home' for elderly people.

The Euston Coffee Tavern was located on the corner of Earle Street and Prince Albert Street, though why it was actually called 'Euston' Coffee Tavern is not clear.

Other Material

Page 52: The portrait by C. H. Charnock is ... ?

Page 52: The portrait by G. Hall Neale is in the Webb Suite near the ??? entrance to the works. Both this entrance and the Webb Suite are now disused, the portrait being the only artefact to be seen in the room during a visit in March 2011. The other version of this portrait mentioned by Spink as being in the British Transport Museum at Clapham is possibly now in the National Railway Museum, York.

Page 52: One bust by Sir Henry Robinson is in Crewe Heritage Centre. It is believed to have come from the Memorial Cottage Hosital. Where is the other one?

Page 52: The four half relief heads are still on the column of the drinking fountain at the entrance to Crewe Park. Three of them are identifiable - Webb, Moon and Lord Stalbridge - but the fourth is uncertain. It is thought to be the 'Commander-in-Chief H.R.H. The Duke of Cambridge', who opened Victoria Avenue, the road which goes past the park.

Page 53: The pattern for the model loco that was on the Boer War memorial in Crewe Park was in the entrance to the Railway Veterans Institute (p54). Where is it now?

Page 52: *Hardwicke* is in the National Railway Museum, York. The 'Coal Tank' No. 1054 is at Ingrow undergoing its second major overhaul. It is expected to be back in action once more in early 2012..

Page 53: Many excellent models now exist in many scales and are far too numerous to list. The large-scale models mentioned are now located as follows:

King Edward VII is in the entrance hall of the Municipal Offices, Crewe. *Jubilee* is in the National Railway Museum, York.

Marchioness of Stafford is in the National Railway Museum, York, but not on display. A photograph of it appears on page 90 of *Model Railway Engines* by J. E. Minns published by Octopus Books in 1973. The caption reads: 'An impressive 9½in-gauge model of ... No. 2798 *Marchioness of Stafford*, built in 1885 with working leaf springs, Joy valve gear and scale-size cab fittings, 26½in high and 101in long.'

Dreadnought was displayed in the Brussels Exhibition in 1910 but was destroyed in the fire which consumed many of the exhibits after the exhibition closed.

Jeanie Deans is first mentioned in an article by Sams in *Railway Magazine* in 1924, which, referring to about 1900, states: 'The present head of Crewe Works [namely, H. P. M. Beames] was finishing off a very fine model of *Jeanie Deans* to a scale of about half an inch to the foot'. H. P. M. Beames certainly built a model of *Jeanie Deans*, though he never completed the tender, but the scale is more like 2in to the foot, about ¹/₆ full size. After Beames died, the model was kept in the house of his son but eventually gravitated to Penrhyn Castle, where Darroch's model of *Orion* was also kept at that time. It was offered for sale by the auction house Bonham's on 23rd July 1997 but was not sold, and was eventually sold by Peter Wilson of Nantwich to its present owner who is believed to be 'somewhere in Yorkshire'.

Page 55: When was the change in title from Loco Superintendent to Chief Mechanical Engineer? C. J. Bowen Cooke, in the preface to his *British Locomotives* dated July 1893, refers to F. W. Webb as the 'Locomotive Superintendent' of the London & North Western Railway. But in the preface to his *Developments in Locomotive Practice* published in 1902 he refers to him as 'Chief Mechanical Engineer'. So the change in title probably took place between those dates.

Plate 1: *'Chief Officers of the London & North Western Railway 1894'. Mr Webb is seated at the right-hand end of the table on the left, with an unrolled drawing on his knee, presumably of an engine. The photograph is possibly some sort of composite created in the dark room from a number of other photographs.*

Plate 2: *Group posed beside the General Offices in Crewe Works, with F. W. Webb and presumably other officers and possibly directors of the LNWR, and the visiting party of Sir Salar Jung, after whom 'Precedent' 2-4-0 No. 858 was named in honour of the occasion. The date must therefore be May 1877.*

Plate 3: *Crewe Memorial Cottage Hospital, 7th May 1896.*   Crewe D3

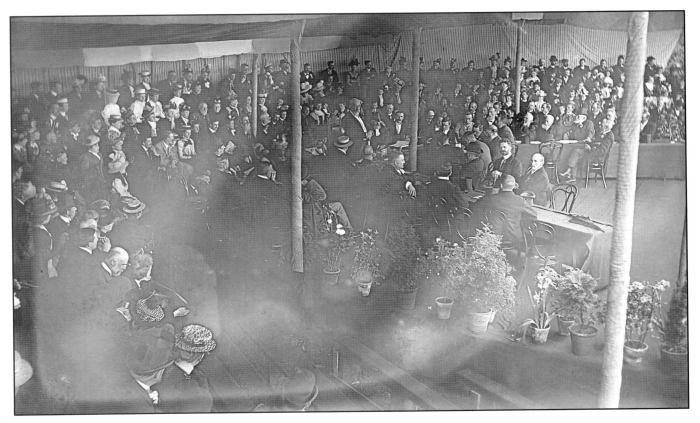

Plate 4: *View inside the marquee at the fete of the Crewe Memorial Cottage Hospital on 14th June 1900. F. W. Webb is addressing the gathering.*   Crewe D63

Plate 5: *Front view of Chester Place, the residence provided by the London & North Western Railway for its locomotive superintendent. Behind the camera is a hedge and then a wall, and at a slightly lower level the path running beside the old Chester line between the General Offices and the Steel Works site.* Crewe C182

Plate 6: *F. W. Webb in the garden of Chester Place with a group of Whitworth scholars and exhibitioners who had gained their awards between 1872 and 1900 while employed at Crewe. Fourth from the left is T. E. Sackfield, who from 1893 was assistant to J. N. Jackson, chief draughtsman at Crewe. Jackson was appointed in 1888 and retired in 1919. Sackfield retired in 1924, so between them these two men supervised Crewe locomotive design from the 'Teutonics' to the end of the LNWR. In the centre of the back row with bow tie is George Ravenscroft, who was manager of the steel foundry at Beyer Peacock for many years.* Crewe A419

Plate 7: *The party at Hartington on the occasion of the opening of the line between Parsley Hay and Ashbourne on 1st August 1899. F. W. Webb is standing on the far right.*

Plate 8: *General view of Queen's Park, Crewe, looking across the lake to the pavilion on the right, and the clock tower and lodges at the main entrance on Victoria Avenue.* Crewe C202

Plate 9: *General view of the clock tower and lodges at the main entrance to Queen's Park, Crewe, looking from within the park towards Victoria Avenue.* Crewe C210

Plate 10: *The Euston Coffee Tavern on the corner of Earle Street and Prince Albert Street. Inside there seem to be nice lamps and statues of charming ladies, more the kind of thing that might be expected in Paris rather than Crewe!*   Crewe A353

Plate 11: ' *A perfect maze of pulleys, straps, shafts and revolving wheels' was Bowen Cooke's description of the fitting shop in the Old Works, photographed here on 30th March 1906.* Crewe A523

Plate 12: *Interior view of the new iron foundry, prepared for its official opening by Richard Moon in May 1882, with many items produced in Crewe Works displayed for the official visitors to see.* Crewe OS135

Plate 13: *Interior of No. 8 erecting shop about 1900, with 'B' class four-cylinder compound 0-8-0s under construction. In the right foreground are frame plates for bogies, for 'Jubilee' or 'Alfred the Great' class 4-4-0s, or '1400' class 4-6-0s.* Crewe A400

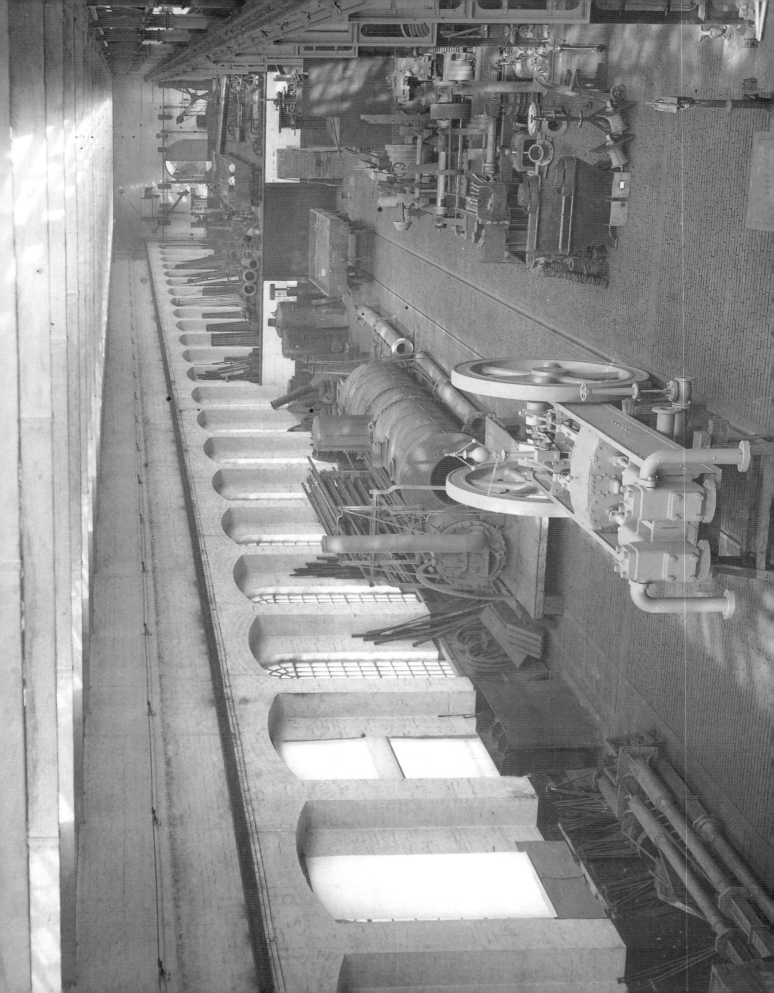

Plate 14, opposite: *General view of the western end of the millwrights' shop, the former foundry, in the Deviation Works, looking west. In the foreground is a hydraulic pumping engine incorporating a 'DX' class cylinder block. To the left of it, against the wall, is the urinal mentioned in Charles Taylor's Life in a Loco Works: First-hand Experiences of a Crewe Engineering Apprentice in Wartime, as being the only indoor urinal in the whole of the Works, and just beyond that is the Trevithick stationary engine brought to Crewe on F. W. Webb's instructions and restored. Further down the shop is single-plank open wagon No. 6780 on a turntable.*

Plate 15, left: *In its historic trial in 1804, on the existing tramway at the Penydarren Ironworks in South Wales, Richard Trevithick's Penydarren engine hauled 10 tons of iron ore and 70 men for 9 ¾ miles from Penydarren to Abercynon, and so became the first example of successful steam operation on track. The ironmaster who bought the locomotive from Trevithick won a 500 guinea bet with a rival iron-master. The story goes that Mr Webb found the engine in South Wales and had the parts brought to Crewe and restored. Whatever, this drawing and pictures of the restored locomotive seem to show a replica.*

Its present whereabouts are not known, but a working replica of Trevithick's Coalbrookdale engine, believed to be simi-lar to the Penydarren engine, works at the Blist's Hill site of the Ironbridge Gorge Museum.

Plate 16, left: *Replica of Rocket, made at Crewe and photographed there on 10th January 1907. So it may well have been a project initiated when F. W. Webb was in charge. It appears in many official pictures in late LNWR and LMS days; its present whereabouts are unknown.. Crewe OS99*

Plate 17, above: *The Trevithick stationary engine, parts of which were found at Hereford, brought to Crewe on F. W. Webb's instructions and restored; it was built by Hazeldine Works, Bridgnorth, about 1814. It is raised off the ground on a wooden platform but even so the flywheel ran in a slot in the floor. Later it was stored in the paint shop and is now in the Science Museum in South Kensington.*

Plate 18: *F. W. Webb's coupé hauled by Trevithick 6ft Single Locomotion, originally No. 138 Bat, on 16th August 1898 with Chester Place visible behind the wall.* Crewe A195

Plate 19: *Eventually, Locomotion was replaced by No. 3020 Cornwall but instead of being renamed Locomotion, it remained Cornwall, the name presumably being considered too famous to be replaced. This view was taken long after Mr Webb had gone, on 5th October 1911. Fortunately, Cornwall still survives in preservation.* Crewe A561

Plate 20: *This is not Mr Webb's coupé but Mr Footner's, the company's chief engineer, which was probably similar inside to Mr Webb's. One difference was that the leading end of Mr Webb's coupé was narrowed, so as to provide a view ahead over the tender and footplate. How much the enginemen appreciated this is not recorded.*   Crewe X13

Plate 21: *A standard type of footbridge, made in Crewe Works and erected beside the paint shop for photography.* Crewe MA141

Plate 22, above: 'STEEL SLEEPER AND CHAIR, F. W. WEBB'S SYSTEM 1885' *set out for photography, probably in the foundry, at Crewe Works.*

Plate 23, below: *Machine for shaping wheels and tyres of locomotives and ensuring they are perfectly circular.* Crewe A307

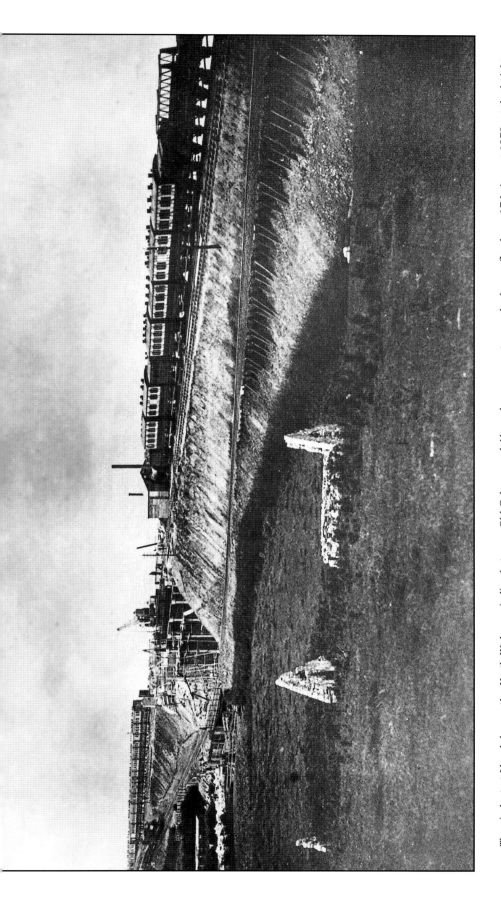

The viaduct at Llandulas on the North Wales main line between Old Colwyn and Abergele was swept away by heavy floods on 17th August 1879, at the height of the holiday season. Nothing could be done to repair the link for two days, as the floodwater was so high, but then a wooden structure on the inland side was built to serve as a temporary replacement and was in operation eight days later on 25th August. Work on a new viaduct was immediately begun. The steelwork for it was completed at Crewe in seven days and consisted of 14 lattice and 28 plate girders, plus flooring plates and angles, for seven 32ft spans.

G. P. Neele, who has an account of the incident in his Railway Reminiscences describes this as 'one of Mr Webb's most notable performances at Crewe Works'. New masonry piers were built by 'Mr Footner's men' (Mr Footner was the chief engineer) and the completed new structure was opened on 14th September.

Plate 25: General view of the new viaduct at Llandulas under construction, looking roughly west. The carriages on both sides of the viaduct are probably to provide accommodation for men employed on the rebuilding work. An up train is descending to cross the temporary bridge at the lower level.

David J. Patrick collection, Crewe A171?

Plate 24, opposite: Here the new steelwork for the viaduct has been erected beside the paint shop in Crewe Works, probably to make sure it all fitted correctly, before being dismantled and transported to Llandulas. The paint shop itself is still quite new, being built in 1876-7 and first used in 1878; the small building with chimney by the paint shop wall housed the heating system which provided warm air to flow through the vents in the pits beneath the engines being painted to help to dry the paint.

Crewe A173

Plate 26 : *Webb-Thompson signal frame in the signal shop. Signal manufacture was originally carried out in the former tender shop at the Old Works but requirements increased so much that a purpose-built signal shop was erected just west of the paint shop in the most northerly row of shops in the Steel Works, parallel to Richard Moon Street, which came into use in 1884.* Crewe A49

Plate 27: *Driving wheels with balance weights in the enlarged centre boss rather than in the conventional position around the rim. The weights were put into pockets or recesses in the inner side of the boss between the spokes. These wheels are on a straight axle – that is, not on the crank axle – and so are the trailing driving wheels. They were for the 'Jubilee' four-cylinder compound which went to the Paris exhibition in 1900, No. 1926 La France and were photographed on 5th March 1900.* Crewe C662

Plate 28: *Hydraulic press for carriage wheels, 1883.* Crewe C22

Plate 29: *A set of engine frames being assembled. The chalked inscription reads: 'No 1 E99 a/c', which means the frames are for the first engine (No 1) of engine account (E) No 99. Engine accounts prefixed with E started in 1869 and went up to E113 in 1883, when they started again from E1. So there were two E99 accounts at different dates. As the photo is dated 31st October 1896, however, it must refer to the E99 account relating to 10 'Coal Tanks' completed in 1897. This was the last batch of 'Coal Tanks', the first of the batch being No. 2350. Engines were built under account numbers prefixed by 'E'; boilers under account numbers prefixed by 'B' and tenders under account numbers prefixed by 'T'. Presumably, other things built in Crewe Works, such as signalling equipment, had account numbers prefixed by other letters. In the foreground is a machine mounted on a four-wheel truck, presumably 18in gauge, and powered by electricity. It is an 'electric rosebitting machine'; a 'rosebit' being a type of drill used for counter-sinking, the name being derived from the fact that it resembled a rose in shape.   LNWR C463*

Plate 30, above: *Six 'Coal Tanks' assembled to test the new bridge over the yard of the Carriage Works at Crewe. The engines are: 796, 1068, 63, 367, 1052 and 158. Although they might seem to be all new engines from the same batch being used for the photograph, in fact only two are from the same batch, so they have either all been in the Works for repair and have just been turned out of the paint shop or have been brought into the works and been painted in photographic grey for the picture, or perhaps a mixture of the two. The shop visible under the right-hand end of the bridge is the carriage repairing shop. The Eagle Bridge across the main line to Chester is off to the right.*

Plate 31, left: *One of the eagles on the Eagle Bridge, photographed on 14th August 1938.*   *L. Hanson*

Although it often goes unnoticed, Crewe had an impeccable history on standardisation from the very early days with the 'Old Crewe' types. John Ramsbottom continued the good work with his 'DX' class of which 863 were built for the LNWR alone. When he needed a shunting engine, he simply took the 'DX' and fitted smaller driving wheels and a saddle tank, and that was it. Mr Webb kept the same engine but fitted his own style coupling rods and splashers, chimney and safety valves (but regrettably, from the enginemen's point of view, not a cab). When he wanted an engine specifically for mineral work, he simply took the saddle tank off the 'Special Tank' and fitted a tender to produce the '17in Coal Engine', and so it went on.

Plate 32, left: *Webb's version of the 'Special Tank'.*

Plate 33, below: *Webb's '17in Coal Engine', of which 500 were built; it is fitted with a 2000-gallon tender (recognisable by the fact that the tank side is as high as the cab sidesheet) that may be new or may be from a Ramsbottom 'Problem' or 'DX'. The dates of these pictures are not recorded but probably about 1876-8.*

Crewe A8.

Plate 35, above: Like other engineers in the nineteenth century, F. W. Webb knew that coupling rods increased friction and that single-driver engines were much more free-running, which was one reason why his three-cylinder compound passenger engines were 'double singles'; why the London & South Western Railway tried an LNWR 'double-single' compound and why Stirling on the Great Northern continued to use single driver engines for main-line work long after other companies were using 4-4-0s and 4-6-0s. So in the 1890s Mr Webb experimented with 'friction drive'. 'Samson' class No. 757 Banshee, when withdrawn, was modified with no couplings but with a friction-drive wheel, as seen here, which could be lowered or raised by the driver as required. When starting or climbing gradients the friction-drive wheel would be raised to transmit the drive from the leading to the trailing driving wheels, in effect converting the engine from a 2-2-2 to a 2-4-0, but on the level under easy steam or downhill, the friction-drive wheel would be lowered, and the engine would run as freely as a single-driver engine. This picture was taken in May 1896. Crewe B57

Plate 34, opposite: 'The London & North Western Railway, F. W. Webb's Exhibit' at the Inventions Exhibition in London in July 1885. Centre piece, of course, is the latest three-cylinder compound No. 2798 Marchioness of Stafford (2798 is its Crewe Works motion number not the running number it received later; it was regular Crewe practice that engines exhibited in this way carried their Crewe motion numbers. Another example is the Webb four-cylinder compound La France, which went to the Paris Exhibition in 1900 as 4000). Behind it is a Webb-Thompson signal frame, while just behind the barrier are, left to right: a specimen of the duplex reverser, which enabled the reversers of both inside and outside cylinders to be operated with one wheel; a model of the first of the class, No. 503 Dreadnought and what looks like some sort of ground signal. The inscriptions on the lamps are hard to determine. The near one on the left seems to be 'Carlisle & the North'; the one on the right, 'Euston'. Crewe C161

Plate 36: *The model of* Dreadnought *which was displayed alongside* Marchioness of Stafford *at the Inventions Exhibition. It was destroyed in a fire in Brussels after being exhibited there as one of the LNWR exhibits.* Crewe A411

Plate 37: *Model of 'Jubilee' class four-cylinder compound 4-4-0 No. 1906* Jubilee. Crewe A407

Plate 38: *A good example of what Tuplin described as 'a neat external style', and Ahrons as 'the simplest and cheapest locomotives ever made in this country', '17in Coal Engine' No. 920 at Ordsall Lane about 1890, though the class commonly ran in this condition from about 1876 to about 1900 (when some were lined out) and well beyond. Ordsall Lane shed is to the right, and the camera is looking north west, across the Liverpool & Manchester main line, carriage sidings, and Bridgewater Collieries sidings beyond. The signal box is one of at least seven at Ordsall Lane.*

Plate 39: *The celebrated 'Jumbo' or 'Improved Precedent' No. 790 Hardwicke photographed at Crewe Works on 29th September 1899. The location is along the old Chester line leading from the General Offices to the Steel Works. Chester Place is beyond the bushes off to the right and behind the camera is the Deviation Works. This photograph merits study by modellers and all who are interested in Hardwicke as it was in the days of F. W. Webb. As now preserved in the National Railway Museum, it has long-taper Cooke buffers which it had when withdrawn by the LMS, rather than the Webb type seen here. It also has LMS-style lamp irons and a numberplate with the incorrect '9', an upside down '6', of the post 1915 type, which it was given when restored to LNWR condition. Finally, in 2011 Hardwicke's cab roof was painted white, perhaps to match another engine with a white cab roof alongside it. What would F. W. Webb say about that?*

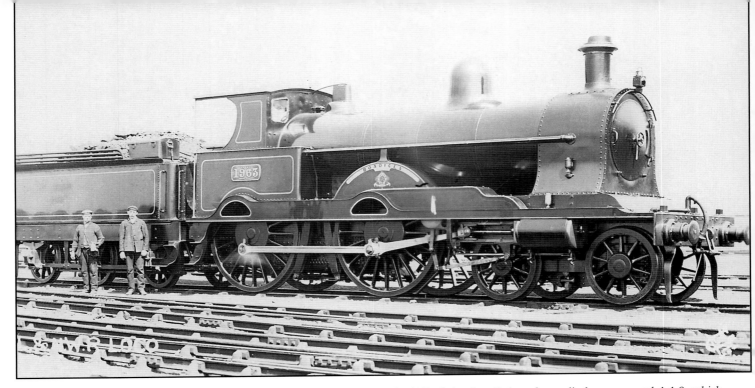

Plate 40, above: *Mr Webb's final express passenger engine was the 'Alfred the Great' class four-cylinder compound 4-4-0, which when modified with separate control of high and low-pressure cylinders as here were capable of producing sufficient power to handle all normal train loads without being piloted. The modified engines were known as 'Benbows' after the first to be so treated. Here, 'Benbow' No. 1963 Boadicea and her crew pose for the camera. The 'neat external design' commented on by Tuplin continued to the end of F. W. Webb's reign at Crewe. A question rarely raised and never answered is who first devised the traditional LNWR lining of red, cream and grey, first introduced at Crewe under F. W. Webb in 1875. Was it Mr Webb himself or someone in the drawing office? We shall never know, but whoever it was deserves the highest praise for a uniquely impressive livery on black paint, that was eventually adopted by British Railways and found to suit many different locomotives from a variety of non-Crewe traditions.*

Courtesy E. Pouteau

Plate 41, below: *The final variant on the Webb four-cylinder compound was the '1400' class mixed-traffic 4-6-0, which came to be known by the nickname 'Bill Baileys'. They had a dubious reputation but were in fact well up to the standard of mixed-traffic 4-6-0s on other railways at the period. Here No. 637 stands at Chester on 21st June 1909.*

K. A. C. R. Nunn collection, courtesy LCGB

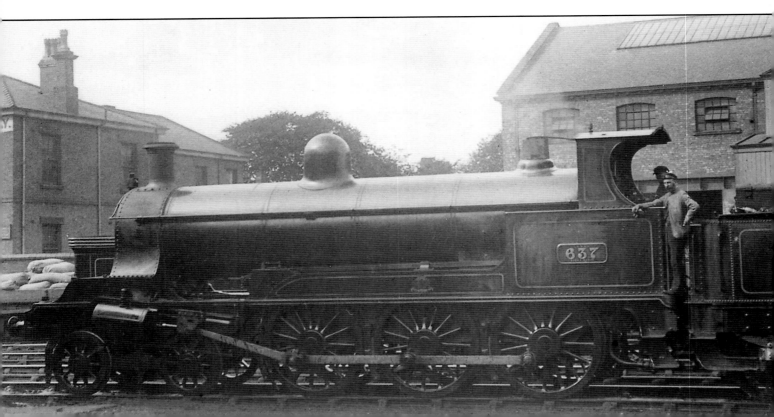

Plate 42: *The Old Rectory Tixall, Staffordshire, in October 2010, where F. W. Webb was born. The house faces roughly east, and from its rooms about four miles away can be seen the North Staffordshire Railway line from Colwich to Stone, opened in 1849. About a mile away to the south is the west end of Shugborough Tunnel, constructed by the Trent Valley Railway and opened in 1847. The building of these railways must have been a source of great excitement in this small rural community, and F. W. Webb, then ten years old, may well have been captivated by these great enterprises.*

Plate 43: *General view of Queen's Park entrance, looking from the roadway towards the entrance off Victoria Avenue. The two lodges are on either side of the entrance gates and the clock tower and drinking fountain is about thirty yards from the gates.*

Plate 44: *One of the lodges by the entrance to Queen's Park.*

Plates 45 and 46: *On the Victoria Avenue side of the lodges, above the first-floor windows in the Vee of the gable roofs are these scenes about 3ft square, one featuring a moon and the other a web.*

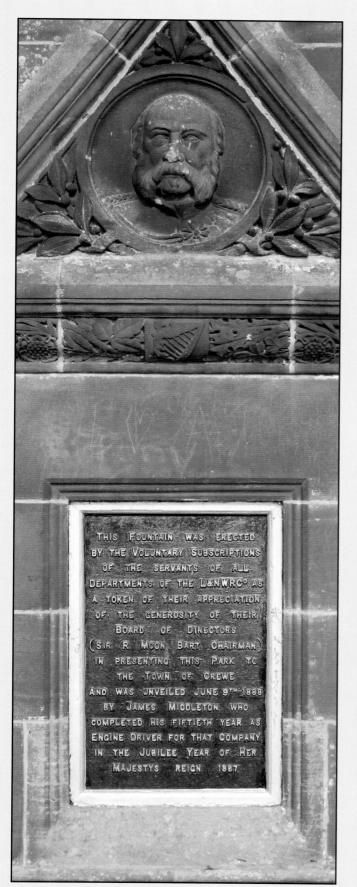

THIS FOUNTAIN WAS ERECTED
BY THE VOLUNTARY SUBSCRIPTIONS
OF THE SERVANTS OF ALL
DEPARTMENTS OF THE L&NWRCº AS
A TOKEN OF THEIR APPRECIATION
OF THE GENEROSITY OF THEIR
BOARD OF DIRECTORS
(SIR R MOON BART CHAIRMAN)
IN PRESENTING THIS PARK TO
THE TOWN OF CREWE
AND WAS UNVEILED JUNE 9TH 1888
BY JAMES MIDDLETON WHO
COMPLETED HIS FIFTIETH YEAR AS
ENGINE DRIVER FOR THAT COMPANY
IN THE JUBILEE YEAR OF HER
MAJESTYS REIGN 1887

Plates 47-49: *Reliefs of heads of James Middleton, Richard Moon and F. W. Webb on the clock tower*

Plate 50: *The roadway from the entrance to Queen's Park leads to the South African War Memorial in which the Crewe Yeomanry, made up of railwaymen volunteers, took part. This model of 'Alfred the Great' class 4-4-0 No. 1942 King Edward VII, which John Spink records as being in a case on this memorial, was removed from this position in the 1990s and is now on display in the entrance to the Municipal Offices in Crewe, as seen here. It is believed to have once been painted in LNWR livery, John Spink describes it as 'gilded bronze' and it is now well polished in that condition.*

Plate 51: *The Webb Orphanage in October 2010. It is situated a little further along Victoria Avenue on the opposite side.*

Plate 52: *Portrait of F. W. Webb. A label beside it states: 'This portrait of Francis W. Webb was painted by J. Hall Neild and is the property of the Railway Benevolent Institution, Electra Way, Crewe, CW1 6HS.*

Plate 53: *The plate attached to the bottom of the frame of the portrait.*

Plates 54 and 55: *On 16th June 1900, when he was elected a Freeman of the Borough of Crewe, F. W. Webb was presented with a silver gilt casket containing an illuminated address. The casket is in the form of a railway carriage, decorated with allegorical motifs depicting Science, Labour, Industry (the beehives) and speed (the caduceus – the wand carried by mythical heralds such as Mercury). On the lid is the coat of arms of Crewe, Webb's crest, and his initials superimposed on a spider's web. On one side of the casket is the inscription explaining its purpose and on the other an enamel picture of Queen's Park. This casket is now preserved in the National Railway Museum, to whom thanks are due for making it available for inspecion and photography.*

Plates 56 and 57: *On the ends of the casket are enamel pictures of the Crewe Memorial Cottage Hospital and of Crewe railway station about 1860, with the Crewe Arms Hotel beyond.*

Plate 58: *The illuminated address contained in the casket.*

Plate 59: *Bust of F. W. Webb, now in the Heritage Centre, Crewe, and the explanatory plaque beneath it.*

Plate 60: *This scene painted by Terence Cuneo is based on a sketch by F. W. Webb and shows two engines which were already 'historic' in Webb's time - Richard Trevithick's Penydarren engine and Francis Trevithick's Cornwall.*

Plate 61: *View of Stanway Manor, Webb's country house near Church Stretton, about 1900.* Courtesy of Shropshire Records and Research Centre

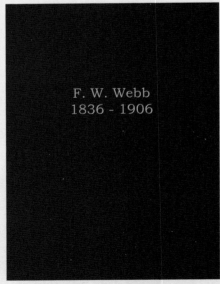

F. W. Webb
1836 - 1906

Plate 62: *Peter Stanton's original copy of John E. Spink's bibliography which this book reproduces.*

Opposite: *Plan of Stanway Manor Estate drawn up by the agent when the property was bought by F. W. Webb. The farm where he installed a railway was not at Stanway Manor itself but at Upper Stanway a few fields away.* Courtesy of Shropshire Records and Research Centre